THE LAW OF WORLDWIDE VALUE

THE LAW OF WORLDWIDE VALUE
by Samir Amin

Translated by Brian Pearce
and Shane Mage

MONTHLY REVIEW PRESS
New York

Portions of this book were originally published as
The Law of Value and Historical Materialism
©1978 by Monthly Review Press

Amin, Samir.
  The law of worldwide value / by Samir Amin ; translated by Brian Pearce
and Shane Mage.
     p. cm.
Includes bibliographical references and index.
ISBN 978-1-58367-234-1 — ISBN 978-1-58367-233-4 (pbk.)
1. Capitalism. 2. Value. 3. Historical materialism. 4. Marxian economics.
I. Amin, Samir. Loi de la valeur et le matberialisme historique. II. Title.
  HB501.A591713 2010
  335.4'12—dc22

                              2010046315

Monthly Review Press
146 West 29th Street, Suite 6W
New York, New York 10001

www.monthlyreview.org
www.MRzine.org

5 4 3 2 1

Contents

Introduction to the English Edition

Marx is not a philosopher, a historian, an economist, a political scientist, or a sociologist. He is not even a scholar of the first rank in any of those disciplines. Nor even a talented professor who prepared a good multidisciplinary dish cooked with all these ingredients. Marx's place is quite outside all that. Marx is the beginning of the radical critique of modern times, starting with the critique of the real world. This radical critique of capitalism demands and allows discovery of the basis of market alienation and, inseparable from it, the exploitation of labor. *The foundational status of the concept of value derives from this radical critique.* It alone allows a grasp of the objective laws that govern the reproduction of the system, underlying those surface movements perceptible through direct observation of reality. Marx links to this critique of the real world the critique of discourses about that reality: those of philosophy, economics, sociology, history, and political science. This radical critique uncovers their true nature which, in the last analysis, is always an apologetic one, legitimizing the practices of capital's dominating power.

To be a "Marxist" is to continue the work that Marx merely began, even though that beginning was of an unequaled power. It is not to stop at Marx, but to start from him. For Marx is not a prophet whose conclusions, drawn from a critique of both reality and how it has been read, are all necessarily "correct" or "final." His opus is not a closed theory. Marx is *boundless*, because the radical critique that he initiated is itself boundless, always incomplete, and must always be the object of its own critique ("Marxism as formulated at a particular moment has to undergo a Marxist critique"), must unceasingly enrich itself through radical critique, treating whatever novelties the real system produces as newly opened fields of knowledge.

The subtitle of *Capital*—"A Critique of Political Economy"— does not mean a critique of a "bad" (Ricardian) political economy, with a view to replacing it with a "good" (Marxian) one. It is rather a critique of so-called economic science, an exposure of its true nature (as what the bourgeoisie has to say about its own practice); and so of its epistemological status, an exposure of its limitations, and an invitation to realize that this alleged science, claimed to be independent of historical materialism, cannot possess such independence. Political economy is the outward form assumed by historical materialism (the class struggle) under capitalism. On the logical plane historical materialism is prior to economics, but class struggle under capitalism does not take place in a vacuum: it operates on an economic basis, and shapes laws that appear economic in character.

I shall study this articulation first as it is presented in *Capital* itself, that is, in the theory of the capitalist mode of production, and then in the reality of the capitalist system of our own day—in imperialism.

My thesis is: (a) that historical materialism constitutes the essence of Marxism; and therefore (b) that the epistemological status of the economic laws of capitalism is such that they are subordinate to the laws of historical materialism; (c) that under the capitalist mode of production economic laws possess a theoretical status different from that which they possess under precapitalist modes; and even (d) that, strictly speaking, economic laws are to be found only under the capitalist mode; (e) that the economic laws of capitalism do indeed exist objectively; and, finally, (f) that these laws are governed, in the last analysis, by the law of value.

Thus, in my view, the class struggle under capitalism in general, and in the imperialist world system in particular, operates on a definite economic basis and, in its turn, changes that basis.

My readings in Marx certainly brought considerable intellectual fulfillment and convinced me of the power of his thought. Still, I was left unsatisfied. For I was asking a central question, that of the "underdevelopment" of contemporary Asian and African societies, and I found no answer in Marx. Far from "abandoning" Marx and counting him "outdated," I simply came to the conclusion that his opus had remained incomplete. Marx had not finished the opus that he had set out to complete, and that included not integrating the "global dimension" of capitalism into his analysis. So I have tried to do so. The central axis of the conclusions reached by my efforts is defined by the formulation of a "law of globalized value," coherent, on the one hand, with the bases of the law of value proper to capitalism as discovered by Marx and, on the other, with the realities of unequal globalized development.

My major contribution concerns the *passage from the law of value to the law of globalized value*, based on the hierarchical structuring—itself globalized—of the prices of labor-power around its value. Linked to the management practices governing access to natural resources, this globalization of value constitutes the basis for *imperialist rent*. This, I claim, orders the unfolding of really existing capitalism/imperialism's contradictions and of the conflicts linked to them, so that classes and nations are imbricated, in their struggles and clashes, in all the complex articulation, specific and concrete, of those contradictions. I claim that our reading of the twentieth and twenty-first centuries can be nothing other than that of the emergence—or of the "reawakening"—of peoples and nations peripheric to the globalized capitalist/imperialist system.

In order to carry out my exposition, I have chosen to take up again my book *The Law of Value and Historical Materialism* in a new, revised and expanded, edition. In the extensive borrowings that I have made from this old (1978) book I have conserved its essential argument. The new paragraphs draw the reader's attention to the challenging questions arising from that retained exposition. If them I have tried to present synthetic explanations which—in themselves adequate—do not preclude coming back to deeper readings.

My theoretical analysis of the really existent globalized capitalist system starts from the law of value formulated by Marx in Volume I of *Capital*. There is no other possible point of departure, because without the concept of value there is no meaning to that of the accumulation of capital—and so we cannot skip over this detour through value in favor of a direct grasp of reality—which is implied by a positivist/empiricist methodology, as revealed through observed prices.

The analysis that I am putting forward thus looks next at the three stages in the transformation of value: (1) into "prices of production"; (2) into "market prices" (oligopolistic prices, in contemporary capitalism); and (3) into "globalized prices" (in the globalized imperialist system).

The first of these transformations, taken up in the first chapters of Volume III of *Capital*, is indispensable to grasping the meaning of the market alienation that governs economic and social life under capitalism and to giving to the laws ruling its systemic reproduction their true stature.

The second of these transformations, that of prices of production into "market prices," had been partially treated by Marx, also in Volume III of *Capital*, in the instance, among others, when he came to consider the distribution of surplus-value in regard to agrarian landownership. We have next to consider the deformations of the price system linked to the emergence of oligopolies/monopolies and above all to take fully into account the gigan-

tic transformation of the system of expanded equilibrium resulting, after the First, but above all after the Second World War,
from the accelerated expansion of a third department—of
absorption of surplus surplus-value. Baran and Sweezy, with the
concept of surplus that they put forward, replied to the challenge
and unhesitatingly extended and enriched Marxian theory. I claim
that those Marxists who still refuse to recognize the central
importance of Baran and Sweezy's contribution lack the means to
put forth an effective critique of contemporary capitalism. Their
"Marxism" thus remains confined to exegeses of Marx's texts.

The central object of my reflections has been the third transformation, which allows us to go from the law of value, taken at its
highest level of abstraction (the capitalist mode of production),
to what I have called the law of globalized value, which is operative on the scale of the really extant polarizing system of capital-
ism/imperialism. It is only this transformation that allows us to
take the measure of the imperialist rent which is at the origin of
the polarization deepened and reproduced by the globalized
unfolding of capitalism.

It is impossible to "understand the world" by a realistic analysis of really existing capitalism outside the framework traced by
the treatment of these transformations of value. Equally, a strategy aiming to "change the world" can be based only on these
foundations. As against this, the positivist/empiricist method of
vulgar economics allows us neither to "understand the world" and
to grasp the nature of the challenges confronting workers and
peoples, nor, a fortiori, to "change" it. Furthermore, that vulgar
economics does not seek to go beyond capitalism, which it sees as
the "end of history." It seeks only to legitimize the basic principles
of capitalism and to show how to manage it.

I believe that this new edition, drawn broadly from *The Law of
Value and Historical Materialism*, comes at the right moment. This
is because the current crisis revolves altogether around different
possible developments of the social and international relation-

ships that govern the form of the law of value, under the combined effects of popular struggles in the central and peripheral
societies of contemporary capitalism and of struggles between
dominant imperialist societies and those of the dominated
periphery—struggles that call into question the continued dominance of what I call "the later capitalism of the generalized, financialized, and globalized oligopolies."

CHAPTER ONE

The Fundamental Status of the Law of Value

After devoting Volume I of *Capital* to the foundations of the law of value, Marx concerns himself in Volume II with what might seem to be a purely "economic" argument. He tries, in fact, to show that accumulation can take place in a "pure" capitalist system, and to determine the technical conditions for dynamic equilibrium.

In Marx's illustrative examples, the system is characterized by a certain number of magnitudes and proportions, all of which belong strictly to the economic field. These magnitudes and proportions are: (a) the proportions in which labor-power and means of production are distributed between the two departments that define the main basis of the social division of labor, making possible the *simultaneous* production of means of production and of consumer goods; (b) the proportions that characterize, for each department, the degree of intensity in the use of means of production by direct labor; this intensity measures the level of development of the productive forces; (c) the evolution from one phase to another of these latter proportions, measuring the pace and direction of the progress of the productive forces; and (d) the rate of exploitation of labor (the rate of surplus-value).

Marx offers a series of examples in which the magnitudes are all given in value terms, and he is right to do so. But what he deduces from these examples—namely the economic conditions for expanded reproduction—could, to some extent, be deduced in the same way from a model constructed directly in terms of prices of production, in which profit is shown in proportion to capital employed and not to labor exploited. Within this precise and limited context, the two arguments, both of them "economic," are equivalent to each other.

There is nothing, then, to prevent one from expressing directly—in terms either of value or of price—the general economic conditions for expanded reproduction by formulating a system of linear equations in which the various variable magnitudes allowed to each department, defined correctly in relation to the parameters of sectoral distribution and of evolution from one phase to the next, are related to each other by the equality in value from one phase to the next in the respective supply of and demand for consumer goods and means of production.

I have done this—in value terms, defining, with the Greek letters lambda (λ) and gamma (γ), two parameters for measuring the progress of the productive forces in each department and from one phase to the next, and then characterizing this progress by the increase in the physical quantity of use-values produced with a decreasing quantity of labor. I therefore set out a model of expanded reproduction (with progress in the productive forces) which is defined simply as follows:

PHASE 1:

Department I: Production of means of production

$$1e + ah = pe$$

(meaning a hours of direct labor, using 1 unit of equipment and raw material, produce p units of equipment).

Department II: Production of consumer goods

$$1e + bh = qc$$

(meaning: b hours of direct labor, using 1 unit of equipment and raw material, produce q units of consumer goods).

PHASE 2:

The progress of the productive forces is defined by the capacity of the same quantity of direct labor (a and b) to set to work a larger mass of equipment and raw material and produce by this means a larger mass of equipment and consumer goods. Or, when λ and γ measure the progress of the productivity of labor (with λ and γ both >1):

$$1e + a\lambda h = pe$$
$$1e + b\gamma h = qc$$

Within this very general framework I established the following set of propositions:

1. A dynamic equilibrium is possible, provided only that labor-power ($a + b$) is distributed between the two departments in suitable proportions.

2. The pace of accumulation (measured by the growth in the production of equipment) conditions the level of employment (a conclusion opposite to that assumed by conventional economics).

3. Dynamic equilibrium presupposes that the consumer goods produced during one phase are purchased during

that same phase and the equipment goods produced during one phase are purchased at the beginning of the next. Since the surplus-value generated during one phase cannot be realized until the next phase, dynamic equilibrium requires centralized and correct management of credit.

4. If the entire economy is reduced to these two departments, dynamic equilibrium demands that there be an increase in wages, to be determined in a proportion that combines λ and γ.

5. If real wages do not follow their necessary progression, equilibrium is possible only if a third department, for unproductive consumption of surplus-value, develops parallel with Departments I and II.

1. An Illustration with a Simple Model of Accumulation

The relation between the two departments of production can be expressed in terms of physical quantities:

$$\text{Department I} \quad 1e + 4h \rightarrow 3e$$
$$\text{Department II} \quad 1e + 4h \rightarrow 6c$$

Constant capital inputs are given directly in capital goods units e, direct labor inputs in hours h; outputs are given in capital goods units e for Department I and in consumption units c for Department II. In this example, it will be noted that the organic composition is the same in both Departments.

It is assumed that the product of labor is shared between the proletarian and the capitalist in identical proportions in the two Departments (identical rates of surplus-value). It is also assumed that wages constitute the sole source of demand for consumer goods c, i.e., that the purchasing power incorporated in the remuneration of labor enables the entire output of Department II to be absorbed during each successive phase described. On the other hand, the entire surplus-value is "saved," in order to finance gross investment (replacement and additions), i.e., the purchasing power incorporated in the surplus-value generated during one phase enables the installation of the capital goods necessary to maintain the dynamic equilibrium of the next phase.

As to dynamic equilibrium, we define the progress achieved between one phase and the next by the rate of increase of labor productivity (the output divided by the input of direct labor). For example, if productivity in each Department doubles between one phase and the next, the technology for Phase 2 will be given as follows:

$$\text{Department I} \quad 2e + 4h \rightarrow 6e$$
$$\text{Department II} \quad 2e + 4h \rightarrow 12c$$

The same quantity of direct labor utilizes twice the quantity of capital goods, raw materials, etc., to produce a doubled output. The physical organic compositions are doubled.

How, under these conditions, can equilibrium be maintained from one phase to the next? Let us assume that the quantity of labor available in the society ($120h$) and available stock of capital goods ($30e$) are given from the outset. Their distribution between the two Departments, the rate of surplus-value and the rate of growth (the surplus production in I over replacement needs) are simultaneously interdependent. For example, we have:

Phase 1	Capital Equipment		Necessary Labor		Surplus Labor		Output
Department 1	$20e$	+	$40h$	+	$40h$	$\rightarrow$	$60e$
Department II	$10e$	+	$20h$	+	$20h$	$\rightarrow$	$60c$
TOTAL	$30e$		$120h$				

Here, the output of Department I during Phase 1 is twice what is necessary to replace the capital equipment and makes it possible to obtain during Phase 2 an output which is itself doubled. We verify that the proportions 2/3–1/3 which represent the distribution of the productive forces between I and II and a surplus-value rate of 100 percent, i.e., unchanged (hence double real wages) are the conditions of dynamic equilibrium, where Phase 2 is expressed in the following way:

Phase 2	Capital Equipment		Necessary Labor		Surplus Labor		Output
Department 1	$40e$	+	$40h$	+	$40h$	→	$120e$
Department II	$20e$	+	$20h$	+	$20h$	→	$120c$
TOTAL	$60e$			$120h$			

Note that the purchasing power incorporated in the wages corresponding to 120 hours of labor (of which $60h$ is necessary labor) should make it possible to purchase $60c$ during Phase 1 and $120c$ during Phase 2, i.e., that real wages should double in the same way as labor productivity. Capital equipment output, being doubled between one phase and the next, finds an outlet in the following phase. We note that the rate of increase of available capital equipment governs the total quantity of labor used and not the reverse. This is a very important point: the accumulation of capital governs employment and not the reverse (as claimed by bourgeois economics in general and marginalism in particular). Here, by the very choice of assumptions, the volume of employment remains unchanged from one period to another. Under the assumption of an increase in the working population, for instance, a natural increase, the rate of accumulation does not make full employment possible.

This very simple model illustrates the nature of the objective relation between the value of labor-power and the development level of the productive forces in the capitalist mode of production. Nothing is gained by using a common denominator so as to be able to add up the inputs, by substituting prices for values in the computation (equalization of the profit rate which is, here in any case, equal to the rate of surplus-value, the organic compositions being the same in both Departments), or by introducing more complicated assumptions: different organic compositions and/or different increases in productivity in the two Departments.

The conditions of equilibrium, for example, can obviously be expressed in homogeneous terms. Assuming the unit price of c to be $1F$, that of e, $2F$, and the wage rate per hour $0.50F$, the surplus-value (here equal to the profit) being obtained as the difference, we have the situation shown in Phase 1. For the following phase, if the money wage rate remains the same, the prices of the products are reduced by half, productivity having doubled (see Phase 2). Note that there is no difficulty of absorption. For the absorption of consumer goods, the wages paid in each phase ($60F$) make it possible to purchase the entire output of Department II in the same phase: in the first phase, $60c$ at $1F$ per unit; in the second phase, $120c$ at $0.50F$ per unit.

Phase 1	Capital Equipment	Wages	Surplus-Value	Output
Department I	$20e \times 2 = 40F$	$80h \times 0.5 = 40F$	$40F$	$60e \times 2 = 120F$
Department II	$10e \times 2 = 20F$	$40h \times 0.5 = 20F$	$20F$	$60c \times 1 = 60F$
TOTAL	$60F$	$60F$	$60F$	$180F$

Phase 2				
Department I	$40e \times 1 = 40F$	$80h \times 0.5 = 40F$	$40F$	$120e \times 1 = 120F$
Department II	$20e \times 2 = 20F$	$40h \times 0.5 = 20F$	$20F$	$120c \times 0.5 = 60F$
TOTAL	$60F$	$60F$	$60F$	$180F$

A useful observation at this point is that the capital equipment produced during one phase does not have the same use-value as did the capital equipment used in its production. With the 20e installed during Phase 1, not 60e of the same type but 60e of a new type were produced. For instance, with steam engines would be produced, not more steam engines, but electric motors. Otherwise, there would be no way to understand how, with the same type of capital equipment, its efficiency would be doubled in the following phase. If the capital equipments were the same, their efficiency would be the same; that is to say, the same ratio of capital equipment to direct labor. If the same quantity of direct labor can set in motion twice the value in capital equipment in order to produce twice as much output, it means that the equipment is different, new, and more efficient.

This observation allows us to distinguish between a model of intensive expanded reproduction from an extensive model. In the latter, the same capital equipment is produced, but in increasing quantity (such extensive expanded reproduction requires for its service a proportionally increased amount of labor). In the—more interesting—intensive model considered here this is no longer necessarily the case. (A general algebraic model of expanded reproduction is formulated in the Appendix to this chapter.)

2. Realization of the Surplus-Product and the Active Function of Credit

From this general scheme of expanded reproduction I have thus deduced a first important conclusion, namely, that dynamic equilibrium requires the existence of a *credit system* that places at the capitalists' disposal the income that they will realize during the next phase. This demonstration established the status of the Marxist theory of money and gives precise content to the Marxist (anti-quantity-theory) proposition that the supply of money adjusts itself to the demand for money (to social need), by linking this social need to the conditions for accumulation. How important this proposition is remains unperceived by those theorists who do not dare to *continue* Marx's work, but prefer to confine themselves to *expounding* it. Moreover, this precise integration of credit into the theory of accumulation is the *only* answer to the "market question" raised by Rosa Luxemburg.[1]

3. GIVEN THE HYPOTHESIS OF UNCHANGING REAL WAGES, IS ACCUMULATION POSSIBLE?

What happens with the equations of expanded-reproduction when real wages do not increase at the same rate as productivity; for example, when the real wage per hour remains unchanged? There are only two sets of mathematical solutions to the problem: an absurd one corresponding to Tugan-Baranovsky's "roundabout" approach, and a realistic one, introducing the consumption of the surplus-value.

Joining in the debates concerning markets and the trade cycle as early as the beginning of the twentieth century, Tugan-Baranovsky considered a succession of phases in dynamic equilibrium is spite of stagnation in real hourly wages in *The Industrial Crises in England*, published in Germany in 1901. The additional equipment produced in the course of each phase, and in increasing quantity as a result of increased productivity, is allocated to Department I in the following phase in order to produce other equipment, capital, and so on indefinitely, while Department II only expands insofar as the use of the additional equipment requires a quantitative increase in labor, since the hourly wage rate remains unchanged. In the next example, where productivity doubles from one phase to the next in each of the two Departments, we have:

Phase 2	Capital Equipment	Necessary Labor	Surplus-Labor		Output
Department I	50e	100h	(25h, 75h)	→	150e
Department II	10e	20h	(5h, 15h)	→	60c
TOTAL	60e	120h	(30h, 90h)		

Phase 3					
Department I	137.5e	137.5h	(17.5h, 120h)	→	412.5e
Department II	12.5e	12.5h	(1.5h, 11h)	→	75.0c
TOTAL	150.0e	150.0h	(19.0h, 131h)		

The utilization of 60e produced in the course of Phase 1 requires 120h of direct labor during Phase 2. The labor, with its real wage unchanged, is able to purchase 60c, which require only 10e and 20h of direct labor. The remaining equipment (50e) will enable 150e to be produced. This equipment will require in Phase 3 an extra labor of 150h, which combine to produce an output in Department II of 75c (which only requires 12.5e and 12.5h). Equilibrium is achieved from one phase to the next in spite of the stagnation in the real hourly wage combined with the growth in productivity (with a doubling in each department from one phase to the next—both in labor productivity and in the physical organic composition). Equilibrium is obtained through a distortion in the distribution of the productive forces in favor of Department I and the increase in the rate of surplus-value, as follows:

	Phase 1	Phase 2	Phase 3
Organic Composition (Index)	30e/120h 100	60e/120h 200	150e/150h 400
Productivity in Department I (Index)	60e/80h 100	150e/100h 200	412.5e/137.5h 400
Productivity in Department II (Index)	60c/40h 100	60c/20h 200	75c/12.5h 400
Distribution I/(I+II)	2/3	5/6	0.91
Rate of Surplus-value (percent)	100	300	690

This "roundabout" solution is absurd since the balance between consumption and capital equipment must be obtained from one phase to the next and cannot be indefinitely postponed. If each phase corresponds to the life of the capital equipment, this period coincides exactly with the "planning" period for investment decisions. Capital goods will be produced in the course of one phase only if in the following phase the output of consumer goods which they bring about finds an outlet. Thus, in fact, if hourly wages are stagnant, there will be an overproduction crisis as from Phase 2, with the equipment produced in Phase 1 remaining unused, while that proportion of it that does get used will only give rise to a reduced demand for labor. This is the Keynesian problem and the source of the Great Depression: the system has broken down (available equipment and unemployment) and can only be started up again by a rise in wages.

Oddly, the Tugan-Baranovsky solution, absurd in a real capitalism, can be envisaged in the hypothetical case of a planned statism, which would have the means to allow itself to push ever outward the consumption horizon that, under capitalism, governs profitability and investment decisions. Indeed, that was the case in the Soviet system during the Stalinist epoch.

The absurd part of it can be avoided if the surplus-value is consumed. In our very simple scheme, the entire surplus-value is "saved"; but if we assume that a constant proportion of it is consumed, there will be no change in the nature of the equilibria. Hence, if real hourly wages remain stagnant or increase at a lower rate than productivity, an increasing proportion of the surplus-value must be consumed in order to maintain a dynamic equilibrium. For there are no "insurmountable" contradictions—the thesis of catastrophic collapse, of a "general crisis," etc.—but only different alternative ways of overcoming them: capitalist alternatives that preserve the essential features of the system and socialist alternatives that go beyond them.

Under capitalism the question is to be answered through one of the three following solutions:

1. The first "solution"—the individual consumption of an increasing proportion of the surplus-value by the capitalist—is not "normal" since competition among capitalists requires "savings" and the ideology of the system, which reflects the features of the capitalist mode, is opposed to it.

2. The second "solution" is one discovered by the central system itself in order to overcome its contradictions. We have already noted that there are no "insurmountable" contradictions—the theory of catastrophic collapse, of "general crisis," etc.—but only different alternatives to overcome them: those of capitalism that maintain the essential features of the system and those of socialism, which supersede them right from the start. Monopolistic competition, the inclusion of "selling costs" in the price of the product, and the subsequent development of tertiary parasitism, which were well described long ago by Chamberlin and Joan Robinson, constitute, as Baran and Sweezy have said, the "spontaneous" solution of the system.[2]

3. The third "solution" involves direct intervention by the state in the absorption: public, civil, and military expenditure. Paul Baran's great intuition was to understand that henceforth the analysis of dynamic equilibrium could not be made within the framework of the "pure" two-sector model but within a new framework—with three sectors (the third sector in fact being the state, consumer of an increasing proportion of the surplus). This analysis, which corresponds to reality, required the introduction of a concept wider than that of surplus-value and directly linked with the productivity of productive labor. The concept is that of surplus.

Does the introduction of these "solutions," the third in particular, remove the objective status of labor-power? The answer is yes, for those who regard this status from an economistic point of view. But in actual fact, these "solutions" remind us only of the existence of a dialectic between subjective and objective forces; for state intervention must be placed within the context of the class struggle that gives it its meaning.

Dialectic does not mean juxtaposition of autonomous elements. Class struggle, in all its varied manifestations outlined here, does not "reveal" the objective necessities of equilibrium by a lucky chance. Class struggle modifies the objective conditions. The model is necessarily unilateral, but reality is not. The results of class struggle alter the conditions of the "model": they act upon the allocation of resources, the rates of growth of productivity, etc. Objective conditions and subjective forces act and react upon each other.

A final remark: the preceding analysis of dynamic equilibrium did not contain assumptions regarding the trend of the profit rate. We will return to this question later, in relation to the stages of the evolution of the capitalist system and the related question of the falling rate of profit. I will not here enter into the discussions

about the "law of the falling tendency of the rate of profit."
Following Paul Sweezy, I have in my turn dared to offer several
reflections going beyond what Marx wrote on the question. Thus
I entered the discussion to suggest that the facts that can be
acknowledged concerning changes in the profit rate be placed in
the context of a concrete historical framework defining successive
phases characterized by particular combinations of the indicators
(*lambda*, λ, and *gamma*, γ) of the growth of productivity in each
of the two sections modeled in Marx's line of argument.

4. FROM PRICES OF PRODUCTION
TO MARKET PRICES

As the competition among segments of capital is enough to
account for the transformation of values into prices of production, we have now to consider a third family of operative realities,
which in their turn transform prices of production into market
prices. The first element to be considered here is the existence of
oligopolies, which wipe out the liberal hypothesis of "competition." These oligopolies, which have defined contemporary capitalism since the end of the nineteenth century, are positioned to

bleed off monopoly rents from the overall mass of surplus-value,
guaranteeing them rates of profit higher than those obtained by
the segments of capital subordinate to them. The contributions of
Baran, Sweezy, and Magdoff have brought about a qualitative
advance in this domain. They alone allow an understanding of the
nature of capitalism in our time, both its tendency to stagnate and
the ways in which it tries to overcome that tendency (especially
financialization).

Extending that analysis, I have put forward the thesis that
the advanced degree of centralization of capital, henceforward
characteristic of contemporary capitalism, made it worthwhile
to speak, for the first time, of a system of generalized, global-

ized, and financialized oligopolies—the basis for the crystallization of a collective imperialism of the triad of the United States, Europe, and Japan.[3]

the triad

The second intervening element in the determination of market prices calls for a theoretical analysis of the functions of the monetary standard. Marx here puts forward an expanded view of great interest concerning the interlinking of the "standard commodity" (gold) and the role of credit in creating and destroying money. I likewise have put forward several theses about this subject under the new conditions in which the metallic standard has been generally abandoned.[4] The fact remains that human societies—on account of their alienation (in this instance, the market alienation proper to capitalism) always need a "fetish." Gold, in the last analysis, remains that of our "modern" world, as is seen at moments of accumulation crisis—our present moment, for example.

gold

A third family of disparate elements, whether they define a general conjuncture (times of easy growth and times of sharpening competition among capitals) or special conjunctions ("new" products versus products whose growth potential is becoming exhausted), enters into the determination of observed market prices.

The absolute empiricism that is the standpoint of vulgar economics, dominant in Anglo-Saxon cultures even more than elsewhere, claims to draw "laws" allowing the understanding of economic life directly from the observation of immediate realities (prices such as they are). Its failure—as our subsequent consideration of Sraffa's model will show—simply reveals the ideological nature of vulgar economics, reduced to chatter designed to legitimize the activities of capital.

vulgar economics

5. The Unavoidable Detour
by way of Value

What does the law of value state? That products, when they are commodities, possess value; that this value is measurable; that the yardstick for measuring it is the quantity of abstract labor socially necessary to produce them; and, finally, that this quantity is the sum of the quantities of labor, direct and indirect (transferred), that are used in the process of production. The concept of the commodity and the existence of the law of value, formulated in this way, are inseparably interconnected.

What does the law of value *not* state? That commodities are exchanged in proportion to their values; and that direct labor is present labor, whereas indirect labor is past labor crystallized in the means of production. (Volume II of *Capital* is based on the fact that the production of the means of production and the production of consumer goods are not successive in time, but simultaneous, this simultaneity defining the social division of labor in its most fundamental aspect.)

Possessing a certain value and being exchanged at that rate are two different notions. Marx says that, in the capitalist mode, commodities are exchanged in accordance with relations defined by their prices of production. Is this a contradiction? Does it mean that making a detour by way of value is pointless? My view is that neither is so.

Prices of production result from a synthesis of the law of value, on the one hand, and the law of competition among capitals, on the other. The first-mentioned factor, the more fundamental of the two, would cause exchange to take place in accordance with value in a mode of production reduced to the sole reality of domination by the commodity, that is, simple commodity production. This mode does not exist in history. The capitalist mode, which cannot be reduced to this, is characterized by the presence, alongside domination by the commodity, of the fragmentation of capital and competition among capitals (and capitalists). Visible reality, in the form of prices of production, results from the combining of these two laws, which are situated on different levels.

We say that prices of production result from the combined action of the two laws. Can this combination be expressed in a quantified transformation formula? In Volume III of *Capital* Marx does this, in his usual way, by giving numerical examples of various possible cases. He does not put forward successive approximations, but confines himself to a first approximation: constant capital stays measured in value, not in price. One can, without difficulty, solve the problem of transformation in an elegant way, without successive approximations, by means of a system of simultaneous equations. Is this operation legitimate? Certainly it is.

It cannot be said that value is a category of the process of production whereas price belongs to the process of circulation. Value and price are both categories of the process as a whole. Actually, value is realized, and consequently exists, only through exchange. It is in this overall process that concrete labor is transformed into abstract labor, and complex (compound) labor into simple labor.

The only condition for transformation is that it should be possible to reduce concrete wage-labor to a quantity of abstract labor. In fact the actual tendency of capitalism is indeed—by subjecting labor to the machine and downgrading labor skill on a mass scale—to reduce concrete forms of labor to abstract labor.

The question of transformation has been obscured by the fact that the writers who first tried to carry through the operation begun in Volume III of *Capital* also wanted to solve a problem that was easily shown to be insoluble: transforming values into prices while retaining equality between the rates of profit resulting from the equations establishing the production prices and that rate of profit expressed in value and derived directly from the rate of surplus-value.

If we abandon this requirement, we find no difficulty in transforming values into prices. Is the fact that the rate of profit necessarily differs from the rate of surplus-value an embarrassing fact? On the contrary, it is normal for these two rates to differ: indeed, this result of transformation is one of the essential discoveries of Marxism.

In the "transparent" modes of exploitation, the rate of exploitation is immediately obvious: the serf works for three days on his or her own land and for three days on the master's. Neither the serf nor the lord is blind to this fact. But the capitalist mode of exploitation is opaque. On the one hand, the proletarian sells his labor-power, but seems to be selling labor, and is paid for the eight hours of work put in, not just for the four that would be necessary for maintenance; on the other hand the bourgeois realizes a profit that is calculated in relation to the capital owned, not to the labor exploited, so that this capital seems to the capitalist to be productive.

I have ascribed fundamental importance to this difference between the transparency of precapitalist exploitation and the opacity of the extortion of surplus-value under capitalism, and have based upon this distinction a series of propositions dealing respectively with (a) the different contents of precapitalist ideology (alienation in nature) and capitalist ideology (market alienation), and (b) the different relations between base and superstructure, with dominance by the ideological instance in all the precapitalist modes and, contrariwise, direct domination by the economic base in capitalist mode. Thereby I have related the appearance of "economic laws," and so of "economic science," to the capitalist mode.

Bourgeois economic science (neoclassical, i.e., vulgar, economics) tries to grasp these laws directly, on the basis of what is immediately obvious. It therefore takes capital for what it seems to the capitalist to be, that is, a factor of production, productive in itself, with labor as another factor of production.

6. Is an Empiricist Approach
to Accumulation Possible?

The strictly empiricist philosophical mind-set of the Anglo-Saxon world, transmitted to all contemporary vulgar economics, means that only observable facts ("prices," such as they are) count toward the direct deduction of "laws" allowing one to understand the mechanisms of the reproduction of the system and of its expansion. For the "professional" economist, an empiricist and nothing but an empiricist, a detour by way of value is burdensome and useless.

One might confine oneself to replying that to understand capitalism means not only to understand its economic laws but also to understand the link between these laws and the general conditions of social reproduction, that is, the way its ideological instance functions in relation to its base. The concept of value is a key concept, enabling one to grasp this reality in its full richness. Those who carry out the reduction, which I here condemn, always end up by conceiving socialism as nothing but "capitalism without capitalists."

However, this argument, though sound, is not the only one available. We will, in fact, see that the empiricist treatment of the question, which "economizes" that "burdensome and useless detour" (for it) by directly apprehending reality as expressed in "market prices," loses itself in a blind alley.

7. Sraffa's Schema

In Sraffa's model the productive system is given (the quantities of each commodity, $1, 2, \ldots i, \ldots n$, and the techniques used to produce them, including the inputs of direct labor), as is the real wage (the quantity of various goods that the hourly wage enables the wage earner to buy). Consequently, the relative prices and the rate of profit are determined in static equilibrium. The difference between the two methods is situated on two planes, which must be carefully distinguished: (a) the substitution of prices for values; and (b) the adoption of a system of production with n branches instead of the two departments specializing in the production, respectively, of equipment goods and of consumer goods.

Let us assume that there are two lines of production, (1) and (2), each of which produces both producer goods and consumer goods, and that a_{ij} = the coefficients of inputs necessary for the production of these goods, p_1 and p_2 = their unit prices; w = the wage rate (the quantities of labor being assigned by the coefficients a_{01} and a_{02}); and r = the rate of profit. We then have:

$$(a_{11}p_1 + a_{12}p_2 + a_{01}w)(1 + r) = p_1$$

$$(a_{21}p_1 + a_{22}p_2 + a_{02}w)(1 + r) = p_2$$

To this system corresponds the following system of values:

$$a_{11}v_1 + a_{12}v_2 + a_{01} = v_1$$

$$a_{21}v_1 + a_{22}v_2 + a_{02} = v_2$$

Let it be remembered that since the two products (1) and (2) are not destined by nature, one for use as equipment and the other for consumption, this system does not describe an equilibrium of supply and demand for each department. The conditions for *that* equilibrium, which are assumed to be achieved, are external to the model.

We define two parameters of improvement in productivity, π_1 and π_2, specific to each of the branches (1) and (2). Let us assume, for simplicity, that it is the same, π, in both cases. Let us go on to assume that the system of values for Phase 1 is as follows:

$$0.2v_1 + 0.4v_2 + 0.4 = v_1$$

$$0.5v_1 + 0.1v_2 + 0.6 = v_2$$

from which we get:

$$v_1 = 1.15, \text{ and } v_2 = 1.30$$

Assuming that the same quantity of direct labor becomes capable of setting to work twice as much equipment and raw material and, for simplicity, in the same proportions a_{ij} so as to provide twice the quantity of end products (that is, if $\pi = 0.5$), we have for Phase 2:

$$0.4v'_1 + 0.8v'_2 + 0.4 = 2v'_1$$

$$1.0v'_1 + 0.2v'_2 + 0.6 = 2v'_2$$

from which we get:

$$v'_1 = 0.58 \text{ and } v'_2 = 0.65$$

The table below will then show the evolution of the system of values obtained with the same global quantity of labor, left unchanged.

The results, meaning the increase in the net product (from 1.00 to 2.00) are independent of distribution (no assumptions having been made regarding wages or the rate of profit).

	Phase 1	Phase 2
Production	$1.0v_1 + 1.0v_2 = 2.45$	$2.0v'_1 + 2.0v'_2 = 4.92$
– Productive consumption	$0.7v_1 + 0.5v_2 = 1.45$	$1.4v'_1 + 1.0v'_2 = 2.92$
= Net Product	$0.3v_1 + 0.5v_2 = 1.00$	$0.6v'_1 + 1.0v'_2 = 2.00$

Rising productivity can be expressed by falling prices while nominal incomes remain unchanged or by nominal incomes' increases with unchanged unit prices. Here prices are doubled:

$$v'_1 = 1.15 \qquad v'_2 = 1.30$$

If, however, we examine the evolution of a system expressed in prices, we have to introduce an assumption regarding *the way income is distributed.*

The previous system, expressed in price terms, namely:

$$(0.2p_1 + 0.4p_2 + 0.4w)(1 + r) = p_1$$
$$(0.5p_1 + 0.1p_2 + 0.6w)(1 + r) = p_2$$

completed by an assumption regarding wages, e.g., that:

$$w = 0.2p_1 + 0.2p_2$$

can be reduced to a system of "production of commodities by means of commodities only" which here is as follows:

$$(0.28p_1 + 0.48p_2)(1 + r) = p_1$$
$$(0.62p_1 + 0.22p_2)(1 + r) = p_2$$

the solutions of which are:
$$p_1/p_2 = 0.93$$

For the next phase the system becomes:

$$(0.4p'_1 + 0.8p'_2 + 0.4w')(1 + r') = 2p'_1$$
$$(1.0p_1 + 0.2p'_2 + 0.6w')(1 + r') = 2p'_2$$

The results (relative prices and rate of profit) will depend on the way that wages evolve. If we assume an unchanged real wage, that is, if

$$w' = w = 0.2p'_1 + 0.2p'_2$$

the reduced system becomes:

$$(0.24p'_1 + 0.44p'_2)(1 + r') = p'_1$$

$$(0.56p'_1 + 0.16p'_2)(1 + r') = p'_2$$

the solutions of which are $p'_1/p'_2 = 0.98$, from which we get the comparative table, established in price terms, given below:

	Phase 1	Phase 2
Production	$1.0p_1 + 1.0p_2 = 2.08$	$2.0p'_1 + 2.0p'_2 = 4.04$
– Productive consumption	$0.7p_1 + 0.5p_2 = 1.24$	$1.4p'_1 + 1.0p'_2 = 2.42$
= Net Product	$0.3p_1 + 0.5p_2 = 0.84$	$0.6p'_1 + 1.0p'_2 = 1.62$
of which, wages	$0.2p_1 + 0.2p_2 = 0.42$	$0.2p'_1 + 0.2p'_2 = 0.40$
and profits	$0.1p_1 + 0.3p_2 = 0.42$	$0.4p'_1 + .8p'_2 = 1.22$

It will be noted that comparison between the two phases is obscured by the fact that the solution of the system gives relative prices, p_1/p_2 and p'_1/p'_2, which differ according to the evolution of wages. We do know, from our assumption, that the system of Phase 2 will enable us to obtain, with the same total quantity of labor, twice as much physical product (use-values) from (1) and (2). But if we assume $p_1 = p'_1 = 1$, we have p_2 unequal to p'_2, since p_1/p_2 and p'_1/p'_2 both depend on the way distribution takes place. Here $p_2 = 1.08$ and $p'_2 = 1.02$.

The net product, which is the measurement of the growth in value that is independent of distribution (in my model, this net product increases in value terms from 1.00 to 2.00), here increases from 0.84 to 1.62 (a growth rate of 93 percent) when we analyze the evolution of the system in price terms, with the given assumption regarding wages.

It is because of these uncertainties in measurement of the development of the productive forces in price terms that we should prefer models constructed in terms of value, the only certain standard.

The major defect of analysis in price terms compared with analysis in terms of value is not due to the "open" character of Sraffa's model (meaning that the dynamic equilibrium of supply and demand for each product—equipment goods and consumer goods—is not formulated as an internal condition of the model but simply assumed to be related externally), in contrast to the "closed" (full circle) character of Marx's model (in which the equilibrium in question is formalized in the model itself). This defect is due to the substitution of prices, which depend on distribution, for values, which do not so depend. This means that the concept of improvement in the productivity of labor (as the measure of the development of the productive forces), which is perfectly objective in Marx's practice (it does not depend on the rate of surplus-value), is no longer objective in Sraffa's model or in any other model constructed in price terms.

Furthermore, the Sraffian framework does not lend itself to analysis of the conditions for dynamic equilibrium, since, unlike Marx's framework, it is not concerned with the equilibrium of supply and demand for each type of product. It is therefore impossible to deduce from it the propositions set out above concerning expanded reproduction. What it offers is a meager empirical model, which serves at best to describe an evolution that has been observed, but not to infer from this any laws of evolution.

A system defined directly in price terms is also perfectly determined—in the sense that relative prices and the rate of profit are determined—once the rate of real wages is given.

But then there arises the question of a standard, which Sraffa, in the Ricardian tradition, defines like this: is there a standard that would leave the net product unchanged while distribution (w or r) changed independently? The answer to this question is no. Let us see why this is so.

Sraffa does not analyze the system as Marx does. He excludes labor-power from the productive process, in order to consider wages not as the value of labor-power but as a distribution category. This is why he describes the system in the following form:

$$(0.2p_1 + 0.4p_2)(1 + r) + 0.4w = p_1$$

$$(0.5p_1 + 0.1p_2)(1 + r) + 0.6w = p_2$$

He further proposes, as we know, that we select as our standard the price of the net product:

$$0.3p_1 + 0.5p_2 = 1$$

With this standard, r and w are in a linear relationship that is independent of p_1 and p_2:

$$r = R(1 - w)$$

With this standard, r and w are in a linear relationship, whereas any arbitrarily chosen standard gives a relationship between r and w that is neither linear nor monotonic, and is described by a curve (see graph on opposite page).

But is this standard any better than others? Not so at all: (a) because this standard presupposes Sraffa's treatment of wages: if the wage is integrated in the productive process as variable capital, the standard varies when w varies: it is no longer independent of prices; (b) because, even in Sraffa's formulation, since the net product changes with the passage of time (the result of growth), the standard is not independent of prices but is elastic.

If then we reintegrate w in the productive process, as we should, whatever the standard being used, we get three equations and four unknowns (p_1, p_2, r, and w). It is still possible to express r as a function of w, but the relation is no longer linear, nor even of necessity a monotonic decreasing one.

The fundamental question underlying the dispute over whether to choose value as the standard, or something else, is that of how to measure, precisely and objectively, the progress of the productive forces.

The value standard, on the other hand, enables us to measure the progress of the productive forces from one phase to another; that was why Marx chose it.

It is not fair to Marx to reduce his proposition that value should be chosen as the standard of prices to the argument that this standard "works"—that is, that with it transformation is possible. The debate on transformation remains secondary, and however much ink it has caused to flow, it is in no sense primordial.

Marx was actually seeking an instrument by which the development of the productive forces could be measured. This instrument is value. In fact, the quantity of socially necessary labor is, in the last analysis, society's only "wealth"—and value is independent of distribution.

This value standard means comparing the progress from one system (0) to another—(1), (2), etc.—along the Y-axis w. Along this axis $r = 0$, and wages w absorb the entire net product. The system that maximizes w for $r = 0$ maximizes income, or else minimizes the socially necessary labor time needed to produce a given amount of use-values. It corresponds, therefore, to more efficient, more highly developed productive forces.

Sraffa's standard, on the other hand, means comparing the systems along the X-axis r. For $w = 0$, $r = R$, and profit absorbs the entire product. Assuming w different from zero does not affect the conclusion since Sraffa cancels the wage by replacing it with the goods consumed by the wage earner. Sraffa therefore compares

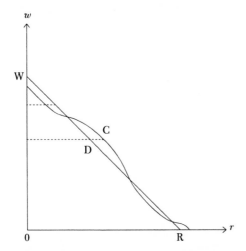

systems along a horizontal line parallel to the z axis, starting somewhere on the vertical w axis. The system that maximizes the rate of profit R will be considered the best. Isn't that the same thing? Not necessarily. The result of the two methods of comparison would be the same only if the two curves (0) and (1) did not intersect. If they do intersect, then it is possible that the system that maximizes w does not maximize r.

Why is this? Because, along the Y-axis $(r = 0)$ comparison between the systems takes into consideration simultaneously (for a system with two products) the four coefficients a_{11}, a_{12}, a_{21}, and a_{22}, corresponding to the commodity inputs, and the two coefficients a_{01} and a_{02}, defining the inputs of direct labor. The productive systems become (for $r = 0$):

$$a_{11}p_1 + a_{12}p_2 + wa_{01} = p_1$$

$$a_{21}p_1 + a_{22}p_2 + wa_{02} = p_2$$

and the prices p are then similar to the values.

If, however, we compare the productive systems along the X-axis for which $w = 0$, this means taking into consideration only the first four coefficients (production of commodities by means of commodities, and not by means of commodities plus direct labor) and leaving out the two coefficients of input of direct labor. The systems then become (for $w = 0$):

$$(a_{11}p_1 + a_{12}p_2)(1 + r) = p_1$$

$$(a_{21}p_1 + a_{22}p_2)(1 + r) = p_2$$

The value standard is superior because this standard alone considers production as the resultant of *all* the technical coefficients that describe it.

The conclusion of this analysis is fundamental: that social system that maximizes the rate of profit (for a given level of wages) does not necessarily maximize the development of the productive forces (the reduction of social labor time).

There is no way of doing without the theory of value. This theory alone enables us to link all the economic magnitudes (prices and incomes) to a common denominator—value, that is, the quantity of socially necessary labor, which is independent of the rules of distribution (exploitation, competition, and so on), and to do this both for characterizing a given phase (static synchronic analysis) and for measuring change from one phase to another (dynamic diachronic analysis) of the progress of the productive forces.

If a single standard is chosen to describe two systems, successive or simultaneous, there is a relation between w and r that is illustrated (see page 41) either by two curves of type C or by one curve C plus one straight line D.

In the system of Sraffa there can exist no common standard for two systems. In that system, wages being replaced by their equivalent (the consumption goods destined for workers), labor disappears from the production equations: commodities are then only produced by means of commodities without intervening labor (which remains underlying); the surplus being entirely attributable to capital, which becomes the only factor of production! We have here reached the highest stage of alienation: commodities (including subsistence goods for workers) have children (a larger quantity of commodities) without the intervention of labor as such. This supreme alienation is comparable to that of the financier who, making money by means of money, regards money as in itself productive (see chapter two). Or, even further, material inputs are made to disappear, replaced by their equivalent in past labor. Then in the system will appear only one factor, dated labor falling back on the factor "productive time" à la Böhm-Bawerk.

All post-Marxian economics has tried—in order to get rid of Marx—to put the origin of "progress" somewhere other than in social labor. To that end, it has invented specific productivities of "the factors of production," or reduced these to that of the "commodity" (Sraffa: "commodities produced by means of commodities"), or to that of money (money produces money), or to that of time ("time is money," Böhm-Bawerk's discounting of the future), or—today—that of "science" ("cognitive capitalism," descended from the marginal efficiency of capital as it was understood by Keynes). All these are nothing but forms of the basic alienation proper to conventional bourgeois social thought.

Marx had filled out his critique of capitalist reality with a critique of the writings that aimed to legitimize capitalist practice, whether those produced by the great classics, who founded modern thought in the domain of the new political economy (Smith, Ricardo), or of those from the vulgar economics already present in his day (Bastiat and others). Critique of the post-Marxian economists is no less necessary. It has been carried out by several good Marxists who have thrown off the yoke of exegesis. In this regard, the contributions of Baran, Sweezy, and Magdoff have been crucial. Let me point here to my own contribution to critique of the best attempts of conventional economics to extend the classics (Keynes, Sraffa) and also my critique of the new forms of vulgar economics (which I called "the witchcraft of modern times").[5]

8. ECONOMIC LAWS AND THE CLASS STRUGGLE

The schema of expanded reproduction thus seems to reveal that precise economic laws do exist, which, like any other laws, have an objective existence, that is, impose themselves willy-nilly on everyone.

To conclude, the importance of Volume II of *Capital, as it stands*, is essential: it shows that, in the capitalist mode, social reproduction appears first and foremost as *economic* reproduction. Whereas in the precapitalist modes, in which exploitation was transparent, reproduction implied direct intervention from the level of the superstructure, that is not so here. This qualitative difference needs to be emphasized.

There has been no question, so far, of the class struggle. This is, indeed, absent from the direct discourse of Volume II of *Capital*.

"Economic determinism" was foreign to Marx, but not so to historical Marxism. A linear economic determinism, linked to a scientistic philosophical vision of "progress," was predominant in the Second International and became even more dominant when social democracy, after the Second World War, abandoned its claim to derivation from Marx.

One attitude that can be taken in this connection is that the class struggle setting bourgeoisie and proletariat against each other over the division of the product (the rate of surplus-value) is subordinate to economic laws. The class struggle can, at most, only reveal the equilibrium rate that is objectively necessary. It occupies, in this context, a position comparable to that of the "invisible hand" of bourgeois economics. The language of the "universal harmony" of social interests is replaced by that of the "objective necessities of progress."

What we have here is a reduction of Marxism to the so-called Marxist (or, rather, Marxian) political economy that is fashionable in the English-speaking world under the name of "Marxian economics." According to this view, there are economic laws, which constitute objective necessities, irrespective of the class struggle.

On such a basis, however, it is no longer possible to conceive of a classless society in the true sense, since it appears as a society identical with class society. The progress of the productive forces continues to dominate it, just as this progress has been dominant throughout history. This progress has its own laws: an ever more intensified division of labor, in the form we know well. Capitalism is seen as guilty only of not being able to carry forward the march of progress effectively enough. As for those writings of Marx in which he criticizes sharply the shortsightedness of the philistine who cannot imagine a future in which no one is exclusively an artist or a lathe-operator, they are so much utopian daydreaming. Capitalism is seen as, basically, a model for eternity, blameworthy only for the social "wastage" constituted by the capitalists' consumption, and for the anarchy caused by competition among capitals. Socialism will put an end to these two abuses by organizing, on the basis of state-centralized ownership of the means of production, a system of "rational planning."

How are we to arrive at this statist mode of production—the highest stage of evolution, a wise submission to "objective laws" for the greater good of society as a whole? By the road of reformism: trade unions, by imposing a "social contract" governing the distribution of the gains of productivity, prepare the way for the formal expropriation of the unnecessary capitalists, after having first served as a school of management for the cadres and elites who represent the proletariat and whose task it is to organize and command.

There is a second possible attitude. Reacting against this type of analysis, one proclaims the supremacy of the class struggle. Wage levels, it is held, result not from the objective laws of expanded reproduction, but directly from the conflict between classes. Accumulation adjusts itself, if it can, to the outcome of this struggle—and, if it can't, the system suffers crisis, that's all.

I here put forward four theses concerning the linkage among the (economic) "laws" of capitalistic accumulation, on one side, and the social struggles, in the broadest sense, on the other. By that, I mean the totality of social and political struggles and conflicts, national and international.

THESIS 1: These struggles and conflicts, in all their complexity, produce "national" systems and a global system, which go from disequilibrium to disequilibrium without ever tending toward the ideal equilibrium formulated by conventional or Marxian (but, in my opinion, scarcely Marxist) economists.

THESIS 2: The inner logic of capitalism—maximization of the rate of profit and of the mass of surplus-value—gives rise to a tendency toward a disequilibrium favoring the possessing classes (the bourgeoisie in the widest sense) at the expense of labor incomes (of all diverse forms). Capitalist reproduction, by virtue of this fact, ought to become "impossible." And in fact, the history of capitalism is not one of "continuous growth," of a "long tranquil river" assuring continuous growth of production and consumption, flowing over accidental obstructions that are called "crises." Like Paul Sweezy, I view this history, contrariwise, as being one of long crises (1873–1945; 1971 to today and, no doubt, stretching far beyond 2010), reducing the short periods of rapid (and problem-free) growth to historical exceptions (like the "thirty great years" between 1945 and 1975).[6]

THESIS 3: Despite this permanent malaise, capitalism has managed so far to get out of its blind alleys and to invent effective ways for adapting to the demands posed by changes in the balance of social and international forces. This reminds us that the progress of the productive forces (its pace and the directions it takes) is not some independent exogenous factor, but one that results from class struggle and is embodied in production relations—that it is modulated by the ruling classes. This thesis reminds us that the Taylorism of yesterday and the automation and "technological revolution" of today are responses to working class struggle, as are also the centralization of capital, imperialism, the relocation of industries, and so on.

So long as capitalism has not been overthrown, the bourgeoisie has the last word in class struggles. This must never be forgotten. It means that unless crises lead to the overthrow of capitalism—which is always a *political* act—they must always be solved in the bourgeoisie's favor. Wages that are "too high" are eroded by inflation, until the working-class, exhausted, gives in. Or else "national unity" makes it possible to shift the burden of the crisis onto others' backs.

For a view of the matter that is not one-sided we need to appreciate that the class struggle proceeds, in the first place, from a given economic situation, reflecting the reality of a particular economic basis, but that, as long as the capitalist system still exists, this modification necessarily remains confined by the laws of economic reproduction of the system. An alteration in wages affects the rate of profit, dictates a type of reaction of the bourgeoisie that is expressed in given rates of "progress" in given directions, changes the social division of labor between the two departments, and so on. But as long as we remain within the setting of capitalism, all these modifications respect the general conditions for capitalist reproduction. In short, *the class struggle operates on an economic base and shapes the way this base is transformed within the framework of the immanent laws of the capitalist mode.*

The schemata of expanded reproduction illustrate this fundamental law that the value of labor-power is not independent of
the level of development of the productive forces. The value of
labor-power must rise as the productive forces develop. This is
how I understand the "historical element" to which Marx refers
when writing of how this value is determined. The only other
logical answer to that question is the rigid determination of the
value of labor-power by "subsistence" (as in Ricardo, Malthus,
and Lassalle).

But this objective necessity does not result spontaneously
from the functioning of capitalism. On the contrary, it con-
stantly comes up against the real tendency inherent in capitalism, which runs counter to it. The capitalists are always trying to
increase the rate of surplus-value, and this contradictory tendency is what triumphs in the end. This is how I understand
what is meant by the "law of accumulation" and the "relative and
absolute pauperization" by which it is manifested. Facts show
the reality of this law—but on the scale of the world capitalist
system, not on that of the imperialist centers considered in isolation; for whereas, at the center, real wages have risen gradually
for the past century, parallel with the development of the productive forces, in the periphery the absolute pauperization of
the producers exploited by capital has revealed itself in all its
brutal reality. But it is there, precisely, that the pro-imperialist
tendency among Marxists pulls up short. For it is from that
point onward that Marxism becomes subversive. (This problem
of the class struggle in relation to accumulation on the world
scale will arise again in chapter four.)

Capital overcomes this contradiction by developing a "third
department," the function of which is to take in hand the excess
surplus-value, which cannot be absorbed in Departments I and II,
owing to the inadequate increase in the real wages of the productive workers. This decisive contribution by Baran and Sweezy has
never been and can never be understood by any of those who

decline to analyze the immanent contradiction of capitalism in dialectical terms.

Starting in the 1930s, but above all since 1945, capitalism has recorded a gigantic transformation that has borne the share of those activities called "tertiary" to heights previously unknown. The reading of this transformation by conventional economists, including Fourastié who was the first to offer an analysis of it, is uncritical—in fact, apologetic. Ours is not.

Undoubtedly the "tertiary" has always existed, if only because no capitalist society is thinkable without a state, whose monarchical functions have a social cost, covered—outside the market—by taxes. Likewise, indubitably, the expansion of "selling costs" associated with the monopolistic competition referred to previously, along with the relative autonomization of commercial and financial activities, are those things at the origin of the accelerated growth of the "tertiary." No less important, however, is the expansion of public services (education, health, and social security) produced by successes of the people's struggles.

So without here going into the labyrinth of the activities called "tertiary"—activities of fundamentally diverse natures—I will here call attention only to the theses that I have put forward concerning the linkage between the puffing up of this "Sector III" of surplus-value absorption and the imperialist fact: the concentration of control operations over the world system by the powers making up the imperialist triad (United States, Europe, and Japan) through what I have termed "five monopolies of the triad's collective imperialism".[7]

Opposed to the strategies of capital, which endeavor to capture control over this swelling of "tertiary" activities through privatization of their management in order to open new fields into which to expand—rather by expropriation than by any new creation—are possible people's strategies of democratic control of the activities in question.

The dizzying expansion of "Department III" (complementing the Departments I and II of the analysis of accumulation put forth in *Das Kapital*), which has become *de facto* "dominant" in the sense that it comprises two-thirds or more of what conventional economics terms GDP (Gross Domestic Product), certainly calls into question the formulations of the law of value that Marx offers us. It is even here that are placed the main arguments in favor of claims that "the law of value is outdated."

THESIS 4: Capitalism only adapts to the exigencies of the unfolding of struggles and conflicts that form its history at the price of accentuating its character as destroyer of the bases of its wealth—human beings (reduced to the status of labor force/commodity) and nature (reduced in the same way to commodity status). Its first long crisis (begun in 1873) paid off with thirty years of wars and revolutions (1914–1945). Its second (begun in 1971) entered the second, necessarily chaotic, stage of its unfolding with the financial collapse of 2008, bringer of horrors and destructions that henceforth are a menace to the whole human race. Capitalism has become an obsolete social system.[8]

9. IS THE LAW OF VALUE OUTDATED?

Identification of value as the central axis for critical analysis of the economy of capitalism and thus of its presence, concealed by the workings of its transformation into observed prices, is not without its problems. Marx's own discussions of these questions invite Marxists not to limit themselves to exegeses of those texts but to dare to go further: in particular concerning (i) concrete labors of diverse character and their reduction to the concept of abstract labor; (ii) the time required for the production, circulation, and realization of surplus-value and, consequently, the relationship between living labor and transferred dead labor; (iii) the identification of use-values; (iv) the treatment of natural resources, whether privately owned or not; (v) the appropriate definition, specific to capitalism, of social labor, and the analysis of its relationship to other forms of labor; and (vi) making clear the forms of absorption of surplus-value by Department III.

The evolution of capitalism since Marx's day and the gigantic transformations that it has produced challenge Marxist analysis. A perspective that tries to stay critical and even to deepen this radical critique of capitalism requires going far beyond Marx's answers to the challenges concerning these questions. Certain Marxists, myself included, are trying to face these challenges.[9]

The current climate of opinion does not favor pursuit of these attempts to enrich Marxism, itself conceived as unbounded in its fundamental critique of the reality of the capitalist world. Instead and in place of enriching Marxist thought, one would rather prefer to bury it and claim to start over from zero. One is then usually the prisoner—whether aware of it or not—of vulgar thought, uncritical by nature. The radical critique of the reduction of the concept of progress to increasing GDP that I have put forward and—in counterpoint—the thesis that I have adopted, likening progress to emancipation, are registered here against the current climate of opinion.[10]

Current fashion is to say that the law of value is "outmoded." It would have applied to the industrial manufacturing phase of capitalism, itself made out of date by the formation of contemporary "cognitive capitalism." Forgotten is that by its essential nature capitalism, today as yesterday, is based on social relationships securing the domination of capital and the exploitation of the labor force associated with it.

The invention of the "cognitive capitalism" concept rests on a capitulation to the method of vulgar economics based on "measurement" of the specific productivities of "factors of production" (labor, capital, and nature). One "discovers" then that the rates of growth recorded by these partial productivities explain only 50 or 60 or 70 percent of the "general progress" (of "growth"). This difference is ascribed to the intervention of science and technology, considered as constituting a fourth, independent, "factor." Some think to have rediscovered in this "factor" the *general intellect*, whose central position in the definition of the productivity of social labor had already been pointed out by Marx. But in fact there is nothing very new there, in the sense that labor and scientific/technical knowledge have been inseparable through all the stages of human history.[11]

There is but a single productivity, that of social labor working with adequate tools, in a given natural framework, and on the basis of scientific and technical knowledge whose elements are indissociable one from the other. What vulgar economics artificially pulls apart Marx unites, thus giving the concept of value that emerges from this unity its fundamental status: the condition in its turn for a radical critique of capitalist reality.

Cognitive capitalism is an *oxymoron*. We will be able to talk of a "cognitive economy" only then, when social relations different from those on which capitalism is based have been established. Instead and in place of this deviant notion inspired by the climate of opinion, I have tried to formulate the metamorphoses that the transformations of capitalism engender in forms of expression of the law of value.

In my work I have imagined a capitalism that has reached the furthest limits of its tendency to reduce the amount of labor used for material production (*hard goods*: manufactured objects and food products) through an imaginary generalization of automation.[12] The departments of production no longer set in motion more than a tiny fraction of the labor force: what is used partly for the production of science and technology (*soft goods*) needed for that of *hard goods* and partly for services linked to consumption. In those conditions, the domination of capital is expressed in the unequal distribution of the total income, and value has no longer any meaning except on this integrated and global scale. The concept of value would persist only because society would still be alienated, mired in scarcity thinking.

Would a system that had reached such a stage of its evolution still merit the appellation "capitalism"? It would probably not. It would be a *neo-tributary* system based on systematic application of the political violence (linked to ideological procedures capable of giving it the appearance of legitimacy) indispensable for the perpetuation of inequality. Such a system is, alas, thinkable on a globalized scale: it is already in the course of being built. I have called it "apartheid on the world scale." The logic of the forces governing capitalist reproduction works in that direction, which is to say, in the direction of making "another possible world," one even more barbaric than any of the class societies that have succeeded each other throughout history.

An Algebraic Model of Extended Reproduction

1. PARAMETERS OF THE SYSTEM

I shall begin with a broad analysis of the system, linking real wages (and surplus-value rates) with the development rates of the productive forces. Each Department (I for production of means of production E and II for production of consumer goods C) is defined, for each phase, by an equation in value terms, as follows:

Phase 1	Department 1	$1e + ah = pe_1$
	Department 2	$1e + bh = qc_2$
Phase 2	Department 1	$1e + a\delta h = pe_1$
	Department 2	$1e + b\rho h = qc_2$
Phase 3	Department 1	$1e + a\delta^2 h = pe_1$
	Department 2	$1e + b\rho^2 h = qc_2$, etc.

The first term of each equation stands for the value of constant capital consumed in the production process, reduced to a physical unit of equipment E, estimated at the unit value e ($e_1 \neq e_2 \neq e_3$, etc.) The second term represents the physical quantity a, b, $a\delta$, $b\rho$, etc., of total direct labor (necessary labor and surplus labor) employed by one unit of E in each Department and each phase. The parameter h measures the value product of one hour of labor (not to be confused with hourly wage). The physical product of each department, p and q respectively, is estimated at its unit value e and c (similarly $c_1 \neq c_2 \neq c_3$, etc.).

The system comprises three pairs of parameters (a, b, p, q, δ, and ρ) and two unknowns (e and c) for each pair of equations that describe one phase. Parameters a and b measure the physical labor intensity in the productive process (their reciprocals are related to the organic compositions), parameters p and q represent the physical product of the productive processes using one unit of equipment E in each Department, and parameter t.

Obviously δ and ρ are less than 1 since technical progress enables us to obtain, with less direct labor, a higher physical product per unit of equipment.

2. Determination of Unit Prices E and C

If we assume $h = 1$, the equations supply the pairs e and c:

$$e_1 = \frac{a}{p-1} \qquad \frac{c_1 = a + b(p-1)}{q(p-1)}$$

$$e_2 = \frac{a\delta}{p-1} \qquad \frac{c_2 = a\delta + b\rho(p-1)}{q(p-1)}$$

$$e_3 = \frac{a\delta^2}{p-1} \qquad \frac{c_3 = a\delta^2 + b\rho^2(p-1)}{q(p-1)}$$

etc.

As the first set of equations shows, as we produce the capital equipment from capital equipment and direct labor, the unit prices of e fall from one phase to the next at the rate of growth of productivity in Department I. On the other hand, consumer goods being produced from capital equipment and direct labor, the unit prices c fall at a rate that is a combination of δ and ρ.

3. EQUATIONS OF EXTENDED REPRODUCTION

If the capital equipment E is distributed between Departments I and II in the ratios n_1 and $1-n_1$, for phase 1, n_2 and $1-n_2$ for the next phase, the equations for the production in value terms are as follows:

Phase 1

D I $\qquad n_1e_1 + n_1aS_1 + n_1a(K - S_1) = n_1pe_1$

D II $\qquad (1 - n_1)e_1 + (1 - n_1)bS_1 + (1 - n_1)b(K - S_1) = (1 - n_1)qc_1$

Phase 2

D I $\qquad n_2e_2 + n_2aS_2\delta + n_2a(K - S_2)\delta = n_2pe_2$

D II $\qquad (1 - n_2)e_2 + (1 - n_2)bS_2\rho + (1 - n_2)b(K - S_2)\rho = (1 - n_2)qc_2$

K is a neutral factor of proportionality.

The dynamic equilibrium of the extended reproduction requires that two conditions be fulfilled:

1. that the wages distributed for each phase (in both Departments) enable the entire output of consumer goods produced during that phase to be bought;

2. that the surplus-value generated during one phase (in both Departments) makes it possible to purchase the entire output of Department I during the next phase.

(a) Equations of supply/demand of consumer goods:

Phase 1 $\qquad n_1 a S_1 + (1 - n_1) b S_1 = (1 - n_1) q c_1$

Phase 2 $\qquad n_2 a \delta S_2 + (1 - n_2) b \rho S_2 = (1 - n_2) q c_2$

(b) Equations of supply/demand of equipment:

Phase 1 $\qquad n_1 p e_1 = e_2$

Phase 2 $\qquad n_2 p e_2 = e_3$

Nominal Wages S are determined as follows:

$$S_1 = \frac{(1 - n)\,[a + b(p - 1)]}{(p - 1)[an + b(1 - n)]}$$

$$S_2 = \frac{(1 - n)[a\delta + b\rho(p - 1)]}{(p - 1)[a\delta n + b\rho(1 - n)]}$$

And Real Wages $S'_1 = S_1/c_1$ and $S'_2 = S_2/c_2$ are:

$$S'_1 = \frac{(1 - n)q}{an + b(1 - n)}$$

$$S'_2 = \frac{(1 - n)q}{a\delta n + b\rho(1 - n)}$$

$S'_2 > S'_1$ since the numerator remains unchanged while the denominator decreases from Phase 1 to Phase 2.

4. NUMERICAL EXAMPLES

Case	1	2	3	4	5	6
Parameters						
a	4	4	4	4	4	4
b	4	8	4	4	4	4
p	3	3	5	5	30	3
q	6	10	6	6	1	6
δ	0.5	0.5	0.5	0.5	1	0.50
ρ	0.5	0.5	0.75	0.75	0.5	1
Prices						
e_1	2	2	1	1	0.14	2
e_2	1	1	0.75	0.5	0.14	1
c_1	1	1	0.83	.83	4.14	1
c_2	0.5	0.5	0.46	0.58	2.14	0.83
Proportion						
n	0.17	0.17	0.15	0.03	0.03	0.17
Nominal Wages						
S_1	1.25	1.14	1.06	1	1	1.21
S_2	1.25	1.14	1.09	1	1	1.14
Real Wages						
S'_1	1.25	1.14	1.28	0.24	0.24	1.45
S'_2	2.50	2.28	2.37	0.47	0.47	1.96

Case 1: Equal organic compositions, equal improvement in productivity in the two Departments.

Case 2: Unequal organic compositions, equal improvement in productivity in the two Departments.

Case 3: Equal organic compositions, unequal improvement in productivity (here $\delta > \rho$).

Case 4:   The reverse assumption to the preceding case $(\delta < \rho)$.

Case 5:   Case 3 tending to be limiting, improvement in productivity being confined to Department I $(\rho = 1/2$ while $\delta = 1)$.

Case 6:   Limiting case of 4—improvement in productivity is confined to Department II $(\delta = 1/2$ while $\rho = 1)$.

CHAPTER TWO

Interest, Money, and the State

1.

In Volume III of *Capital* we find that Marx's language undergoes a sudden change. It is no longer a question of commodity fetishism and alienation, or of the value of labor-power and surplus-value. Marx speaks to us now of social classes as they appear in concrete reality—of workers, industrial capitalists, moneylenders, landowners, peasants, and so on—just as he speaks to us of incomes as they can be perceived directly, through statistics—such as wages, the industrialist's and the merchant's profit, the rate of interest, ground-rent, and so on. It is the moment when he begins to go beyond political economy and to develop his argument in terms of historical materialism.

2.

What Marx has to say about money and interest is scattered through various parts of his work. In the drafts for *Capital* (espe-

cially the *Grundrisse*) Marx gives us a series of reflections that are
as concrete as can be: observations on the policy regarding dis-
count rates followed by the Bank of England or the Banque de
France at particular moments of history, critical thoughts relat-
ing to the commentaries of the principal economists of the time
on these policies, and so on. No explicit theory is expounded in
Volume III, however. Marx puts before us a theory of the rate of
interest that runs like this: (a) interest is the reward of money
capital (not of productive capital); (b) it is therefore a category
of distribution; (c) the rate of interest is determined by the inter-
play of supply and demand for money capital, in which two subclasses, lenders and borrowers, confront each other; and (d) this
rate is indeterminate and can be situated at any point between a
floor (zero interest) and a ceiling (a rate of interest equal to the
rate of profit).

This theory seems to me inadequate. Indeed, Marx does not
show any particular fondness for resorting to "supply and
demand," and when he does so he usually raises at the outset the
question: what real forces determine this supply and this
demand? Here, however, we find nothing of the sort. The theory
is inadequate, in the first place, because the floor and the ceiling
in question are too low and too high, respectively. The rate of
interest cannot be zero because, if it were, there would be no
lenders. It cannot be equal to the rate of profit, for then the productive capitalists would cease to produce, and so they would
not borrow.

Above all, however, it is inadequate because the resort to pos-
tulating two subclasses of capitalists, imagined as being independent of each other, contradicts Marx's thesis on money. Marx considers the demand for money, the social need for a certain quantity of money, as being determined *a priori* by the conditions of
expanded reproduction, with lines of production and prices
determined independently of the quantity of money available.
This rigorously anti-quantitativist position has not only been

accepted by all Marxists, it has morover been continued and made more precise in relation to the schemata of expanded reproduction (see chapter one). It suggests, moreover, that the supply of money adjusts itself to this need, this demand. The creation and destruction of credit by the banking system fulfills this function. If that is the case, one cannot see how the confrontation of supply and demand could in any way determine the rate of interest. We do not observe two independent subclasses meeting in a market for lending and borrowing. What we do observe is, on the one hand, those who demand—namely the productive capitalists as a whole, their demand being dependent on the extent to which their own capital is insufficient—and, on the other hand, institutions that respond to their demand. What do these institutions represent? They do not represent a subclass, that of the bankers. Even if the banks are private establishments, and even if the bank of issue to which they are subject, since it is the ultimate lender, is also a private establishment, state policy has always intervened (even in the nineteenth century) to regulate this supply of money. The monetary system of capitalism has always been relatively centralized. The point is that the bank, like the state, represents the collective interest of the bourgeois class. The "two hundred families" who held shares in the Banque de France were not merely money-lending capitalists; they also constituted, through this bank, the principal nucleus of the French bourgeoisie. Thus, we have here a contrast not between two subclasses but between the capitalists as individuals in rivalry with one another (the fragmentation of capital) and the capitalist class organized collectively. The state and the monetary institutions are not the expression of particular interests counterposed to other particular interests, but of the collective interests of the class, the means whereby confrontation among separate interests is regulated.

3.

The radical critique of political economy initiated by Marx grasped right away the reality of the "real economy/financial image" duality proper to capitalism. Capitalism is not expressed solely through private property in the real means of production (factories, inventories, and other such things). It is equally expressed through ownership instruments relative to these "real" properties. The joint-stock-company offers the classical example of the mode of financialization associated with the circulation as commodities of these ownership instruments. The real capital/fictitious capital duality is thus not the result of a "deviation," still less of a "recent deviation." Through it, even at the beginning, was made manifest the alienation specific to the capitalist mode of production. That alienation puts in the place of the productivity of social labor—the only objective reality—the productivity of separate "factors" of production among which, of course, is capital, assimilated to ownership instruments.

This association of the two faces—real and "fictitious"—of accumulation is begun in Volume III, but Marx intended to develop the discussion of this question in the following volumes, which he did not live long enough to write.

The alienation of the modern capitalist world, like that of earlier epochs, separates "soul from body" and assigns to the soul (today, property) predominance over the body (today, labor). Our modern left, alas, prisoner of empiricist positivism (in particular the Anglo-Saxon variety) and simultaneously allergic to Marx, is by that very fact ill-equipped to grasp the immanence of this duality and of unavoidable financialization.

Financialization is thus in no way a regrettable deviation, and its explosive growth does not operate to the detriment of growth in the "real" productive economy. There is a whole lot of ingenuousness to propositions in the style of "social democracy taken seriously" that suggest controlling financial expansion and mobilizing the "financial surplus" to support "real growth." The tendency to stagnate is inherent in the monopoly capitalism superbly analyzed by Sweezy, Baran, and Magdoff. Financialization then provides not only the sole possible outlet for surplus capital, it also provides the sole stimulus to the slack growth observed, since the 1970s, in the United States, Europe, and Japan. To roll back financialization would thus merely weaken yet further the growth of the "real" economy. Simultaneously, this inescapable financialization increases the fragility of the global equilibrium and multiplies the instances of "financial crises" which, in turn, are transmitted to the real economy. Monopoly capitalism is of necessity financialized; its reproduction goes from "bubble" to "bubble." A first bubble necessarily bursts as soon as the pursuit of "unlimited" growth is hampered for any reason; and the system can get out of the financial crisis occasioned by this bursting only by fabricating and inflating a new bubble.

Analysts from the "critical left" (those unwilling to sign up openly to social liberalism) believe themselves able to propose policies capable of "regulating" capitalism and forcing it to take into consideration the legitimate social demands of workers and citizens. They fear being called "unrealistic radicals" (or even "Marxists"!) were they to come up with anything more. But it is their propositions that are completely unrealistic, for reasons given by Baran, Sweezy, and Magdoff in their precocious analyses of "financialization," which they grasped at its very beginning in the 1980s.

The financial collapse of 2008 has occasioned a flood of disinformation, organized by the dominant media with the help of "experts," accusing the banks of having "abused deregulation," of having "made errors of judgment" (subprime mortgages), even of dishonesty—thus distinguishing and whitewashing the "good capitalists" who are innovators and who invest in real production. Such dissociation is meaningless; the same oligopolies dominate quite equally places of production and financial institutions. Even worse, this dissociation proceeds from a "theory" that knows not that a class state can function, precisely as a class state, only by placing itself above the interests of particular parcels of capital so that—especially through finances—the collective interests of capital should prevail. "Regulation" is the name given to this permanent and unavoidable state intervention.

This regulation takes place in two domains where the collective interest of the class has predominance. The first is regulation of the trade cycle and the second is regulation of international competition.

4.

Regulation of the conjunction does not signify suppression of the cycle but, on the contrary, an ordered intensification of its scope, as a means whereby to maximize the pace of accumulation in time of prosperity and then to control this through liquidations, restructurings, and concentrations in times of crisis. This form of regulation is given ideological expression in the monetarist theories of the conjuncture—that is, in the attempt to rationalize the bourgeois practice of competition. The rate of interest appears as the supreme instrument for this regulation.

When the state acts through the monetary system to impose an increase in the rate of interest, the central authority is intervening actively in economic life in the collective interest of capital. The raising of the rate of interest intensifies the crisis, multiplying bankruptcies. But it thereby accelerates the process of concentration of capital, the condition for the modernizing of the apparatus of production and the conversions that have become necessary. Contrariwise, the reduction in the rate of interest accelerates the growth rate and enables the economy in question to derive maximum benefit from its restored external competitiveness.

5.

The second domain is that of competition among national capitalisms. In the nineteenth century, in Marx's time, the rule of the game where international competition among the central capitalist formations was concerned was that of the gold standard (dual convertibility, internal and external). The flow this way and that of the yellow metal therefore responded to the differences among interest rates. This flow constituted a source, positive or negative, of the supply of money at the disposal of the national monetary institutions. The practicing of monetary policies—that is, the manipulation of rates of interest—was therefore a means of intervening in the conduct of relations among the different national formations. Here, too, increasing the rate of interest in times of crisis helped to reestablish the external equilibrium when this was threatened during the conversion period, by attracting into the country "floating" capital from abroad.

The methods of managing international competition are no longer those known and criticized by Marx. The abandonment of the gold standard and the generalization of flexible exchange rates on the one hand, and the puffing up of the Department III for the absorption of excess surplus-value, on the other, have simultaneously imposed and allowed extreme diversity in economic and financial policy methods. These interventions are based on a healthy dose of empiricism: there is "what has worked" and what has not. But they likewise deploy a vast repertory of "theories," ranging from Keynes to Hayek and on to Chicago monetarism. They continually reformulate models that claim to integrate the "givens" provided by observation and, consequently, to guarantee the efficacious working of the policies envisaged on that basis. To extend the critique that Marx began of the bases and methods of vulgar economics requires, in turn, the critique of all these post-Marxian theories emerging from the field of vulgar economics.[1]

Naturally, study of the domain of international competition cannot be reduced to abstract analysis of the mechanical relations linking different economic magnitudes, national and foreign: the volume and price of imports and exports, the flow of capital and its response to the rates of profit and of interest, and so on. In this domain it is always possible to claim that one can derive economic laws from empirical observation of the facts. Thousands of econometric models have been constructed with this end in view, but the results obtained from them have proved meager. In most cases, the laws inferred from observation of the past cannot be confirmed in the future and do not endow the public authorities with effective instruments of control. The reason for this is that what is essential often lies outside these models: the rate of progress of the productive forces, the results of the class struggle, and the effects of the latter upon the former.

It is my opinion that the reason why Marx did not construct an economic theory of international relations is to be sought here. As we know, Marx did say, in the *Grundrisse* and in several other preliminary sketches for *Capital*, that there would be a chapter on international relations, but he never wrote such a chapter. Was this because he did not have the time? I think, rather, that he gave up his intention because he realized that no economic theory of world trade was possible. Before tackling the economic aspect of international relations (the "economic appearances," the visible part of the iceberg), it was necessary to carry out a thorough analysis in the terms of historical materialism. Just as an analysis of the class struggle on the scale of the national formations had provided the basis for the theory of the capitalist mode, so an analysis of the class struggle on the scale of the world capitalist system is a prerequisite for an analysis of the world economy. But an "economic" theory of international relations is impossible.[2] After rejecting the economic theories of adjustment of the balance of payments, I myself decided in favor of a line of research directed at the class struggles on a world scale, which shape the structural adjustments among national formations within the framework of which the apparent economic laws operate. I had occasion to come back to the problem when I examined the questions of historical materialism and their relation to the law of value operating on the scale of worldwide accumulation.[3]

6.

The two domains—the internal conjuncture and external competitive capacity—are closely linked. This is why the instrument of monetary policy is still the instrument *par excellence* of the economic policy of the bourgeois state.

Here, then, are two domains in which forces are at work that determine the rate of interest: two domains that belong to the realm of historical materialism, not of economics. Economic theory (meaning *pure* economic theory—that is, a science independent of historical materialism) ignores the state, the collective expression of the bourgeoisie, and the national states of the central bourgeoisies that are in conflict with one another. But Marxism never fails to take into account these aspects of social reality, and never deals with them in isolation from an economy that is supposed to ignore them.[4]

Bourgeois economistic ideology has produced, in this domain, dozens of theories, thousands of models, and as many recipes and schools of thought. But the characteristic feature of all these theories, and the reason they remain ideological, is that they avoid the role played by crisis in the restoration of order (because one must not cast doubt on the harmonious character of capitalist growth, crisis has always to be presented as something accidental) and also the nature of the struggle over shares in domination of the world (because bourgeois ideology counterposes economics, where peaceful competition is supposed to reign, to politics, which is admitted to be the scene of evil aggressive behavior).

Undoubtedly, too, the precise content of these theories has had to be adapted, more or less, to the actual evolution of the system. The changes in the predominant forms of competition (the formation of monopolies), the interpenetration of industrial and financial capital, the disappearance of internal convertibility into precious metals, the organization of international monetary blocs—all these phenomena, which figure in the analysis of imperialism, have modified the rules of the money game and the relations between the internal and international conjunctures.

It remains true that the supreme purpose of this economistic ideology is to construct a general model of monetary equilibrium, completing the model of real equilibrium as constructed by Walras.

The method of historical materialism is the very opposite of that which is promoted by research directed toward general monetary equilibrium. This is so, not because it ignores monetary techniques and policies, but because it goes further, placing these techniques and policies in their setting, as instruments of the bourgeois state in the internal and international class struggle.

CHAPTER THREE

Ground Rent

1.

We know that Marx took over Ricardo's theory of differential rent. This was not an example of "marginalist" reasoning. Marginalism assumes that production varies through the association of increasing doses of one factor with another factor, whose quantity is fixed. Here, the same dose of total social labor (with the same proportion of direct and indirect labor) gives different results depending on the quality of the soil (which, not being homogeneous, is therefore not a factor). Marx, too, as we know, developed the theory of differential rent in the same spirit, by introducing an intensive "Rent II" to complement the extensive "Rent I." By doing so he showed himself to be aware that fertility is not something natural, but results from the labor invested in what may be called "the production of soil"—a fact well known to agronomists and to everyone familiar with country life, but continually overlooked by economists both classical and neoclassical.

It is hard to deny that differential rents exist. But the explanation that they are determined by the difference between the productivity of labor on a given plot of land and the productivity of labor on the worst plot has not always carried conviction. An author who claims to be Marxist, Henri Regnault, has tried to build a theory of rent based upon the determination of agricultural prices by average conditions of production, just as in industry.[1] The good-quality plot of land thus receives a positive differential rent, while the poor-quality one (poor in relation to the "average" plot) receives a negative differential rent. The latter is possible only if it comes as a deduction from an absolute rent that is greater in amount. Differential rents are thus presented as resulting from transfers made from the owners of worse plots to the owners of better plots. On this basis Regnault proposes a reconsideration of the analysis of "external economies."

This is certainly a stimulating reflection. But what is truly the point of Marx's argument (and Ricardo's)? What worries Regnault is that, as he sees it, this argument brings in "demand" in a way that is unusual with Marx. I do not agree. I think that the argument is based on different grounds—namely, on whether or not the average conditions are reproducible. If the average conditions are indeed reproducible (crystallized in equipment that can always be acquired) then the capitalists receive super-profits—and not rents (not even monopoly rents)—that are positive or negative depending on whether they use equipment that is superior or inferior to the average. But if we are dealing with the natural conditions of production, that is, by definition, with conditions that are *not* reproducible (over and above the degree to which they may be modified, as envisaged in Rent II), does not the concept of an "average" vanish?

However that may be, whether we are concerned with industry (reproducible means) or with agriculture (non-reproducible conditions), demand enters into the matter in both cases, and in the same way. When a productive system is given (and it matters little here whether it be expressed in values, as with Marx, or in prices, as with Ricardo and Sraffa), this presupposes that production be adequately adjusted to demand: the quantitative distribution of the production in excess of productive consumption needed between each product 1. . . . , *i* . . . . , *n*, corresponds to an equivalent distribution of demand between wage-earners and capitalists (including in this the demand resulting from expanded reproduction). Marx does not eliminate use-value and does not fall into a way of looking at things that is based one-sidedly upon exchange-value.

2.

However, what interests us here is absolute rent, that which is paid for the worst land (*not* marginal land). Marx relates the existence of such rent to that of a class: the landowners.

Is the level of this rent determined? If so, why and how? Marx might have used an argument here similar to his argument about interest, saying that absolute rent is indeterminate and results from the confrontation of two classes, the landlords and the capitalists, with merely a floor—zero—and a ceiling—a level of absolute rent that absorbs all the surplus-value.

Why not? For we know that rent is a category of distribution, since the landowner plays no part in the process of production. Obviously, each of these two forms of transfer income has its own status: if the landowners were to refuse to lease their land then no production could take place whereas, if money were to disappear, it would be re-created. The soil forms part of the *natural* conditions of production; money is one of its *social* conditions.

Apart from that, though, the same argument could be advanced. It would incur the same criticism, namely that the floor is too low (with zero rent the land would no longer be made available for renting) and the ceiling too high (if rent absorbed the whole of surplus-value the capitalists would stop producing).

The question seems to be, then: is rent determined by some economic law that forms part of the whole system of laws governing price formation, or by a pure and simple relation of power? Actually, this question is badly put and needs to be replaced by another: how does this class struggle (between landowners and capitalists) operate on a given economic basis and how does it modify that basis? Only thus will the two domains, that of economics and that of the class struggle, not be separated but be taken together, so defining here, as elsewhere, the true domain of social science: historical materialism.

Yet Marx here gives a simple answer to the question of how rent is determined, one that refers to economic reality only. He affirms that it is the difference in the organic composition of capital, which is lower in agriculture, that determines the value retained by the landowner. I have already said that I find this proposition unacceptable,[2] both on the empirical plane (is the organic composition in agriculture always lower? why so? and if it were *higher* should the rent be negative?) and on the plane of logic. As regards the latter, even if the organic composition were higher in agriculture, could not the rent imposed by landownership act so as to distort prices (as compared to prices of production without rent) just as competition among capitalists distorts prices of production (as compared with values)? In that case, though, are we slipping into indeterminacy?

3.

So far as I know, only one writer, Regnault, attempting to substitute a different economic determination for that offered by Marx, has tried to link rent with the rate of interest. This is his key argument presented in the form of an imaginary discourse: "You own the capital, I own the land. You can take a lease of my land, while I can borrow your capital, in return for paying the rate of interest.

If you invest 100, you will gain $100r$ (r being the rate of profit). If I borrow 100, I gain $100(r - i)$. For the lease of my land I require you to pay me $100(r - i)$."

Regnault concludes that absolute rent results from the existence of a capital market wherein the rate of interest is lower than the average rate of profit. He also notes that this determination must not be confused with the determination of the price of land by capitalizing the rent.

What worries me here is that the capitalist who agreed to pay a rent equal to $100(r - i)$ would no longer be making the average profit r. Why, then, should he choose to invest in this branch, if he cannot add the average profit to his costs of production? Why would he agree to give up his status as a capitalist (receiving r) and be satisfied with that of a money-lender, receiving $r - (r - i)$, that is, i? Though the problem has been shifted back, it is still there.

4.

Most Marxists who have concerned themselves with the question of rent—among those who are not content merely to expound what Marx wrote—have inclined toward indeterminacy on the economic plane, after rejecting determination by comparative organic composition. All we can deduce from a Ricardian, neo-Ricardian, or Sraffian system into which absolute rent has been introduced (which Ricardo refused to do, but which, as we have seen from Marx, can be done) is that rent and profit are inverse functions one of the other. Economic theory cannot explain the *level* of this rent—cannot tell us what determines it.

It seems, indeed, undeniable that the levy upon the net product constituted by absolute rent modifies relative prices and reduces the rate of profit just as an increase in wages does. (We know that relative prices and the rate of profit depend on the level of wages.) This fact can be proven by using either Marx's transformation schemata or a Sraffian model.

Let us take, for example, a transformation schema with two branches, (1) and (2), a rate of surplus-value of 100 percent, and different organic compositions. Without absolute rent, the transformation schema, in the case of the illustrative example set out in the table below, gives a rate of profit of 28.5 percent and prices p_1 = 38.5 and p_2 = 51.5.

SURPLUS PRODUCT

	Constant capital	Variable capital	Form surplus value	Form Profit	Values	Prices of Production
	(1)	(2)	(3)	(4)	(5)	(6)
Branch (1)	20	10	10	8.5	40	38.5
Branch (2)	30	10	10	11.5	50	51.5
Total	50	20	20	20	90	90

If, now, we assume that branch (1) has to bear an absolute rent of 4 (in value $\rho = 4$) for an average rate of profit proportional to capital advanced (30 and 40, respectively) we have:

Branch (1) $p_1 = 30(1+r) + 4(\rho = 4)$

Branch (2) $p_2 = 40(1+r)$

and: $p_1 + p_2 = 90$

which gives: $p_1 = 40.9, p_2 = 49.1,$ and $r = 23$ percent

There is, of course, no reason why the levy represented by absolute rent should be determined in advance and in value terms. All that can be said is that, if it exists $(\rho \neq 0)$, then, on the one hand, it entails a modification of relative prices and of the average rate of profit, and, on the other hand, its magnitude could be determined in real terms, like wages, as a function of the prices themselves, in the general form:

$$\rho = ap_1 + \beta p_2$$

It is also possible, of course, to include rent in a Sraffian schema and arrive at the same conclusions. Absolute rent expresses a social relation and cannot be determined by a simple, natural, economic law.

It seems to me, however, precisely for that reason that this critique stops just at the point where the problems start to become interesting. What I see as important is how rent is determined in the domain of historical materialism—for it is indeed determined in that domain.

Historical materialism, as has been said, cannot be reduced to a games theory detached from its economic basis. It is not a formal exercise enabling us to decide the point of equilibrium between two or among three partners (bourgeoisie and proletariat, or these two classes plus the landowners) who are in rivalry over the sharing of a given cake.

5.

Before turning to this analysis, however, I think it is relevant to recall that Marx already replied to this problematic in his own way, both in *Capital* and in some other, "political," writings.

After determining rent by comparative organic composition, Marx moves on and in the chapters that follow examines the history of rent. What does he do then? He forgets all about organic compositions, makes no further allusion to them, does not even try to give any indication of what they are. Moreover, he stops talking about landowners in general and speaks instead, when he is dealing with England, of "landlords," whom he counterposes to "farmers," and, when he is dealing with France, of "peasants." Here we enter right into the realm of historical materialism.

The case that Marx studies, that of England, is rich in lessons concerning his method, the way he determines rent in the realm of historical materialism. So long as the class of landlords shared power with the bourgeoisie in England (and here we see once more the state intervening in order to widen the "economic" domain), a high rent cut off part of profit. This rent was determined by the division of labor between agriculture and industry, which had to be maintained so long as the English economy was obliged to feed its workers without importing cereals (this being practically forbidden by the Corn Laws). It can be shown that, in order to meet the requirement of equilibrium of supply and demand for agricultural products, on the one hand, and industrial products, on the other, the economic system assigned a given level to rent. If it rose above that level, accumulation in industry would be slowed down and then the supply of grain would be greater than the demand. If it fell below that level, the opposite process would ensue.

This example shows that Marx did not exclude the structure of demand from his analysis, though he did not reduce this analysis to a "general equilibrium" à la Walras, which is merely a static description and—as an explanation—mere tautology. Marx transcends the problem by envisaging dynamic equilibrium. Rent, determined immediately by a confrontation between classes, operates on the basis of economic laws, of an economic reality in which equilibrium of supply and demand is inescapable.

We have seen how Marx integrates demand into the process of accumulation, and how the dynamic equilibrium of supply and demand for production goods and consumer goods is what closes the system, determining at one and the same time, on the basis of a given real wage (the value of labor-power), the relative prices and the rate of profit. This first model comprised only two classes (proletarians and capitalists) and two forms of income (wages and profits). The closing of the system implied a certain distribution of labor-power between Departments I and II—that is, an adequate mode of division of labor, in conformity with the structure of demand.

Let us continue this same line of reasoning, after introducing absolute rent $\rho = f(p_1 p_2 \ldots)$. If the technical data of production (material inputs and inputs of direct labor) and the real wage (the value of labor-power) are given, and if we know also what the rent is spent on (say, for instance, it is wholly spent on luxury goods), then for a given system there is only one level of rent that makes dynamic equilibrium possible. The position is the same, *mutatis mutandis*, as with wages. If the rent rises any higher than that level, then profit is reduced and growth slows, affecting the labor market so as to reduce wages. Conversely, if the rent falls below that level, this entails a crisis of realization: excessive profits foster an increase in production that cannot find an outlet, if the level of wages remains unchanged.

The model includes thenceforth three classes and three types of income. The struggles and alliances among these three classes operate on the basis of an economic system that is defined by adequate modes of the division of labor, and in their turn, as we have seen, where two fundamental classes are concerned, these struggles and alliances modify the conditions in which the system functions.

The class struggles do modify this economic basis. How, in fact, did the English bourgeoisie succeed in reducing the rent charged by the landlords? By abolishing the Corn Laws and substituting for English wheat American wheat, which paid no rent (since there were no landlords on the other side of the Atlantic). It was thus by establishing a new alliance of classes, between English capitalists and American farmers, that the English bourgeoisie freed itself from its local adversary. In its turn, this redistribution of forces modified the division of labor. In England it made possible accelerated industrialization, and in America accelerated development of agriculture. On the scale of the entity "England-America," the economic laws of equilibrium between supply and demand reappear—"without rent."

When, in contrast to this case, Marx analyzes the case of France, he starts from the alliance between the bourgeoisie and the peasants. Here, there were peasants, who owned their land and their equipment and exploited wage-labor only marginally. Marx refrains from splitting the peasant into three beings—the landowner, the capitalist, and the proletarian—in the way that our neoclassical economists later presumed to do. Marx knows that what is involved here is a peasant mode of production articulated with and dominated by the capitalist mode. He knows that, in this peasant mode, production for subsistence remains important, but also that domination by capital compels the marketing of part of the product. The alliance between the bourgeoisie and the peasants (an unequal alliance, in which the bourgeoisie was in command, but an alliance nonetheless, directed against the proletariat) found expression in the agricultural policy of the French state (protectionism and other measures permitting agricultural products to be sold at a relatively high price). It may be that this policy resulted in the peasants' standard of living being higher than that of the proletarians—the comparison is difficult to make. But it is pointless to give the name of "rent" to the difference between the total income of the peasants (their subsistence plus what they got for the produce they marketed) and the sum of the counterpart of their labor and the reward of their capital. Here again, this alliance had "economic" effects, and it functioned on the basis of a division of labor that was different from the division prevailing in England.

Gradually, as the proletarian danger retreated (after 1871, and with imperialist expansion) the bourgeoisie attached less importance to its alliance with the peasantry. It took steps to reduce agricultural prices and ended, though belatedly, by aligning the reward of peasant labor with the value of labor-power. The stress laid by an entire line of research in France upon the "formal domination"[3] that deprived peasant proprietorship of its content (since this proprietorship no longer conferred the right to a pseudo-rent) finds here the objective conditions that have enabled it to develop systematically. Colonial settlement, and the social-democratic hegemony over the proletariat that accompanied it, facilitated this evolution. Settlement in Algeria benefited from the availability of "lands without owners" (owing to the laws expropriating the Algerians) and Algerian wine, which paid no rent, made it possible to lower the income of French winegrowers.

6.

This line of analysis of rent alone seems to me to be capable of placing the problem of the determination of rent correctly in the realm of historical materialism.

From this point of view, the French school—before it gave up on Marxism—brought some very fine contributions to the analysis of the submission of the "independent" peasantry to dominant capital. It also, into the bargain, dealt analytically with "urban ground rent" in analogous terms, thereby enriching Marx.

As for our contribution, we refer the reader to our previous writings.[4] This contribution, concerned above all with the linkage/domination between the capitalism of the imperialist epoch and the peasant modes of the periphery, represents thus a transition to the continuation of our discourse, which takes as its objective putting the method of historical materialism to work as an instrument of analysis, no longer of the capitalist mode (and of the central formations) but now of the global capitalist system (the central and peripheral formations in their mutual relationship).

CHAPTER FOUR

Accumulation on a Global Scale and Imperialist Rent

I now take up what, among the metamorphoses of value, seems to me to be—by far—the most consequential, operating in decisive fashion in all the fields of social struggle and in international and national political conflicts of the modern world. I mean *the transformation of value into globalized value.*

I had "sniffed out" the importance of this question in the course of writing my doctoral dissertation (1954–1956), even though it took me a decade to express, in a still-clumsy way, a first formulation of it. This was not a question posed by Marx. So it is in that precise sense that I will claim—without false modesty—to have contributed to extending and enriching Marxism. The thesis has scarcely been convincing to the thinkers of Western Marxisms, with the exception, as far as I know, of Paul Sweezy, Harry Magdoff, and Giovanni Arrighi. Contrariwise, it has been well received in Asia and Africa where, by diverse but finally converging paths, it has contributed to fashioning an Asian and African face of Marxism, to the emergence of a veritable "shoreless Marx."[1]

The argument is simple, though twofold.

Historical capitalism, as it has really existed, has always been imperialist in the very precise sense that the mechanisms inherent to its worldwide spread, far from progressively "homogenizing" economic conditions on a planetary scale, have, on the contrary, reproduced and deepened the contrast, counterposing the dominant (imperialist) centers to the dominated peripheries. In this asymmetry is affirmed, with violence still greater than that contemplated by Marx, the law of pauperization that is indissolubly linked to the logic of capital accumulation.

Still, despite this permanent asymmetry, capitalism is one and indivisible. Capitalism is not the United States and Germany, with India and Ethiopia only "halfway" capitalist. Capitalism is the United States and India, Germany and Ethiopia, taken together. This means that labor-power has but a single value, that which is associated with the level of development of the productive forces taken globally (the *General Intellect* on that scale). In answer to the polemical argument that had been put against him—how can one compare the value of an hour of work in the Congo to that of a labor-hour in the United States?—Arghiri Emmanuel wrote: just as one compares the value of an hour's work by a New York hairdresser to that of an hour's labor by a worker in Detroit. You have to be consistent. You cannot invoke "inescapable" globalization when it suits you and refuse to consider it when you find it troublesome!

However, though there exists but one sole value of labor-power on the scale of globalized capitalism, that labor-power is nonetheless recompensed at very different rates. Certainly, variations in the price of labor-power do exist within the central capitalist countries themselves: but their amplitude is multiplied tenfold on the global scale.

We can thus model the expressions of this reality and, starting with them, measure, if we want to take the trouble, their amplitude—which is to say, the amplitude of the transfer of value from the peripheries to the centers: A transfer that is hidden behind the observed price and wage system, and as such unthinkable for vulgar empiricist economics. So I will, in the first part of this chapter, formulate the terms of the modeling needed to grasp the metamorphosis of the law of value into the law of globalized value. The second series of arguments concerns access to natural resources, the norms governing their administration, and how they are used. We are here no longer "in" the law of value, but at its frontiers.

That is why Marx does not confound "value" with "wealth," as do all the vulgar economists, including supposed Marxists "open" to the "contributions" of conventional economics. Marx concludes his radical critique in *Capital* with the affirmation that capitalist accumulation is founded on the destruction of the bases of all wealth: human beings and their natural environment.

It took a wait lasting a century and a half until our environmentalists rediscovered that reality, now become blindingly clear. It is true that historical Marxisms had largely passed an eraser over the analyses advanced by Marx on this subject and taken the point of view of the bourgeoisie—equated to an atemporal "rational" point of view—in regard to the exploitation of natural resources. So we have to go back and take up this question from point zero. Of course, bourgeois economics was forced to take into consideration the "price" of access to those resources that could be privately owned, and so conceived an "extractive rent" ("Mining Rent") analogous in its way to ground rent. Henceforward we recognize that the challenge is on a quite different scale, which must deal in an integrated way with the totality of resources that are not to be privately owned. As we will see, vulgar economics cannot do this while the enrichment of shoreless Marxism makes it possible.

The question of the treatment of natural resources is inseparable from the analysis of asymmetric globalization resulting from capitalist expansion. For unequal access to the utilization of planetary resources constitutes in its turn the second dimension, no

less important than that following from the globalized hierar-
chization of labor-power prices and imperialist rent. So we will
take up these questions in the second part of this chapter.

1. THE GLOBAL HIERARCHY
OF THE PRICES OF LABOR POWER

The world system does not appear to lend itself to formalization
in algebraic terms. It is, in fact, made up of segments that appear
heterogeneous and even incongruous: groups of capitalist firms
producing commodities by means of more or less efficient techniques and employing wage-labor at various rates of real remuneration; zones that seem to be precapitalist, where products, not
all of which are marketed, are produced in the setting of various
peasant modes, with or without extortion of surplus labor in various forms (ground rent, tribute, and the like); groups of natural
resources (minerals), access to which is more or less obstructed,
depending on the laws of the states concerned—on whether or
not they appropriate the resources. Furthermore, no world economy can be analyzed without considering the states; these exist
not only on the plane of political reality but also on the economic
plane. The economic exchanges among these states have to balance; there are national monetary systems, some of these are
linked with others, and so on.

Any attempt at translating this set of realities into a system of
equations seems to be a long shot. Even summing up a system
regarded as being close to a pure capitalist mode in a model,
whether Marxian (with Department I and Department II
expressed in values) or Sraffian, constitutes a simplification that
must be surrounded with many precautions.

I do not think, however, that resort to relatively simple
schemata must be ruled out. Each of these schemata will possess
some value, not merely pedagogic but scientific (even though

such value is necessarily limited)—provided that we define precisely what data we are using and realize what these data signify.

Here is an example. One can define a system in which commodities $1 \ldots, i \ldots, z$ are produced, some by means of techniques characterized by material inputs A^c_{ij} and quantities of direct labor L^c_i, and others by means of other techniques characterized by inputs A^p_{ij} and quantities of labor L^p_i. This system can be characterized as follows: (a) a single rate of profit r, the only regulator of distribution throughout the system; (b) a single price P^i for each product i; (c) two different wage levels W^c and W^p ($W^c > W^p$). Certain commodities (1 to m) have, under these conditions, a lower price if they are produced with techniques ($A^c_{ij} L^c_i$), others (n to z) with techniques ($A^p_{ij} L^p_i$), it being understood that those produced according to the first formula pay the wages W^c, and the others pay the wages W^p, and that in every case the capital receives the same reward r.

This system might illustrate (without explaining) the conditions of reproduction (equilibrium between supply and demand, and so on) in a model reflecting a certain reality, namely: (a) all products are world commodities (these commodities have only one price—that which is obtained under the conditions that make it the lowest); (b) capital is mobile on the world scale; (c) labor is *not* mobile, and obtains different rewards at the center and at the periphery. In other words, it is a schematization of the way the production process has been turned into a world process in the imperialist epoch.

A model of this kind can be expressed either in Sraffian terms or in terms of value. It is not a substitute for historical materialism, any more than the schemata in Volume II of *Capital* are. But it is useful because it makes explicit what seems to be an objective economic law in such a system, and therefore a basis upon which historical materialism can operate.

If we accept the data of the system and try to stay within its framework, we are obliged at the outset to ask three questions.

First, why in the peripheral zone do they not combine the techniques $A^c_{ij} L^c_i$ with the wages W^p, which would give a higher profit than can be received with the techniques $A^p_{ij} L^p_i$? Second, why in this case doesn't all capital migrate from the center to the periphery? Third, at a given moment, the distribution of techniques being what it is, is the international division of labor that results from it (the center specializing in branches of production l to m, the periphery in n to z) compatible with equilibrium in exchange, since the fractions of products l to m exchanged for products n to z, at prices pi, ought to be equal?

Economic theory endeavors to answer these questions, and fails. I have examined the various theories produced to explain the equilibrium of the balances of payments (theories of price effects or exchange effects), have shown the circular character of these arguments (based on the quantity theory of money or on assumptions regarding elasticities of demand that presuppose the result), and have concluded that they amounted to nothing more than an expression of the ideology of universal harmonies.[2] But when economic theory, turning away from these nonsensical notions, speaks of "re-equilibrating" income effects, it hits the nail on the head. By so doing, however, it invites us to ask the real question, which sits outside its own field: how are the structures adjusted to each other—that is, by the effect of what forces does this adjustment take place? (What is involved here are class struggles on the world scale.)

The model illustrates one possible case: the case in which labor is not exploited uniformly—that is, when the rates of surplus-value are unequal. In order to introduce this hypothesis (it is, at this stage, no more than a hypothesis) we need to construct the model in terms of values, rather than directly in price terms.

Unequal exploitation is manifested in unequal exchange. Unequal exploitation (and the unequal exchange that results from it) dictates inequality in the international distribution of labor. It distorts the structure of demand, accelerating self-centered accumulation at the center while hindering dependent, extroverted accumulation in the periphery.

2. One Accumulation Model, or Two?

I have proposed two accumulation models, one involving the center and the other the periphery.[3] The model involving the center is governed by the articulation of *Capital*'s two Departments, I and II, which, by that fact, expresses the coherence of a self-centered capitalist economy. Contrariwise, in the periphery model, the articulation that governs the reproduction of the system links exports (the motive force) to (induced) consumption. The model is "outward-turned" (as opposed to "self-centered"). It conveys a "dependence," in the sense that the periphery adjusts "unilaterally" to the dominant tendencies on the scale of the world system in which it is integrated, these tendencies being the very ones governed by the demands of accumulation at the center.

Of course, each of the models (central and peripheral) has gone through successive phases that have their own characteristics. For example, the peripheral model passes from a primary stage (export of agricultural and mineral products) to a stage of industrialization through import substitution (the general model for the second half of the twentieth century, the "Bandung era,") and then to a stage of generalized industrialization with exports competitive to the center's industries (the Chinese model of the 1990s). Nevertheless, the model remains peripheral in that it is inscribed within unilateral adjustment to the demands of globalization.

These conditions, governing accumulation on a world scale, thus reproduce unequal development. They make clear that the underdeveloped countries are so because they are super-exploited and not because they are backward (if in fact they have been retarded, that is what permitted their super-exploitation).

This view, moreover, is confirmed by experience. All projections in constant prices of dependent development policies end up with blockage by a double deficit: of the balance of payments and of the government budget; all current-price (relative prices of imports and exports) projections of those policies arrive at this same blockage even more rapidly. This fact has but one explanation: that the structure of prices is deformed (as an effect of combined class struggles on the world scale) in a way that favors aggravated exploitation of the periphery.

"Catching up," in the sense given to this expression by the false "stages of growth" theory, becomes impossible within the framework of "really existing capitalism," imperialist by its very nature. This conclusion does not apply solely to the past: it challenges the construction of the future. The idea that the so-called emerging countries have embarked on a catch-up path thanks to their deepened integration into globalization such as it is (and it cannot be otherwise) is baseless.

The "two models," nonetheless, constitute but a single reality, that of accumulation operative on a world scale, and characterized by the articulation of Marx's Departments I and II—grasped henceforward at the global scale and no longer at the scale of societies at the center.

For the periphery's exports, at this scale, become constitutive elements of constant capital and variable capital (whose prices they lower), while their imports fulfill functions analogous to those of Department III: that is to say, they facilitate the realization of excess surplus-value.

3. Social Struggles and International Conflicts in a Global Perspective

The model does not imply that the openly capitalist form of exploitation becomes general throughout the system. The system merely assumes commodity production, and that the commodities produced are world commodities. Although introducing a rate of profit r in each equation corresponding to a particular branch of production suggests a generalization of the capitalist form, that condition is not necessary for the logic of the model. We could, for example, retain the rate r for branches of production n to s while excluding it from branches t to z. That would mean that commodities n to s, produced in the periphery, are produced by capitalist enterprises (and in this case we could also introduce here techniques $A^c_{ij}L^c_i$, with the rate of wages W^p), whereas commodities t to z are produced by noncapitalist modes but are subjected to capital through their integration in the market. Here we come upon "formal domination." It is easy to show that, in this case, the amount of surplus labor appropriated by the dominant capital is even larger—that is, the super-exploitation is even greater.

Now we can (and must) go beyond the model, which continues to be economic in character. Now, correctly, we bring in the class struggles.

Going beyond the model means, first, taking into account the historical origins of the system. This implies that we are able to define and analyze the precapitalist modes, to observe and analyze the effects of capital's domination of these modes, and so on. Contributions such as those made by Frank, Arrighi, and myself are meant to serve this fundamental purpose. In no case, though, are they more than beginnings. In this sphere, where very little work has so far been done, there is a need for partial, even daring, theses. The discussion has divided us and will go on dividing us, but the progress we are making is clear, because the anti-imperialist problematic is common to us all.

Going beyond the model means, second, appreciating that there are no economic laws that are independent of the class struggle. That is why I have declared that there can be no economic theory of the world economy. For this reason too, I believe, Marx did not write his chapter on the world economy.

Nevertheless some writers, homesick for economics, try to construct such a theory.

Going beyond the model thus means trying to interrelate the class struggle on the world scale, and to make this interrelation operate on an economic base, explaining how these struggles modify this base, in what direction, and so on. This is what I am trying to do, and this is undoubtedly the essential contribution furnished by the Marxists of the Third World—which is, as a rule, poorly understood and badly received in the West. Without repeating all these analyses here, let me recall that I make distinctions among: (a) the imperialist bourgeoisie, which dominates the system as a whole and concentrates to its own advantage a substantial proportion of the surplus labor generated on the world scale; (b) the proletariat of the central countries, which enjoys increases in real wages more or less parallel to increases in the productivity of labor, and, on the whole, accepts the hegemony of social democracy (these two phenomena are interlinked, resulting from the historically completed structure of capitalism with self-centered accumulation, and are bound up with imperialism); (c) the dependent bourgeoisies of the periphery, whose place is defined by the international division of labor and whose anti-imperialist activity modifies this division; (d) the proletariat of the periphery, subjected to super-exploitation by virtue of the incomplete character of the capitalist structure, its historical subordination (its other-directed type of accumulation), and the disconnection derived from this between the price of its labor-power and the productivity of its labor—and which, consequently, is the spearhead of the revolutionary forces on the world scale; (e) the exploited peasantries of the periphery, sometimes subject to dual, articulated exploitation by precapitalist forms and by capital, sometimes directly exploited by capital alone, through formal subordination—thus always super-exploited, and as a result the proletariat's principal potential ally; (f) the exploiting classes of the noncapitalist modes organized in relation to the foregoing.

This extremely simplified presentation illustrates the fact that the principal contradiction, that which governs all the others and the vicissitudes of which largely determine the objective conditions in which the others operate, is the one that counterposes the peoples of the periphery (the proletariat and the exploited peasantry) to imperialist capital and not, of course, the periphery as a whole to the center as a whole.

In the first place, these struggles determine directly and simultaneously the relative prices at which exchange takes place between center and periphery, and the structure of the international division of labor. They determine the orientation and the pace of accumulation at the center, in the periphery, and on the world scale. They thereby condition the struggles waged at the center.

These struggles take place in a domain defined by contrasts and alliances that change from one place to another. The social-democratic alliance (hegemony of imperialism over the working classes at the center) is a constant all through the history of capitalism, except for possible moments of crisis when it can no longer function. Leadership of the national liberation alliance (of proletariat, peasantry, and at least part of the bourgeoisie) is disputed between the popular classes (in which case the entire bourgeoisie goes over to the enemy) and the bourgeoisie (which then succeeds in making imperialism accept new forms of the international division of labor).

These struggles and alliances thus determine (a) the rate of surplus-value on the world scale and the respective (differing) rates at the center and in the periphery; (b) the surplus labor extracted in the subordinated noncapitalist modes; (c) the price structure of the world commodities through which this surplus-value is redistributed (and, in particular, is distributed between imperialist capital and the capital of the dependent bourgeoisies); (d) real wages, on the plane of their world averages and on that of their averages at the center and in the periphery respectively; (e) the amount of rent drawn by the noncapitalist classes (especially in the periphery); (f) the balance of exchange between center and periphery; and (g) the flow of commodities and capital (and consequently the rates of exchange).

The framework of analysis in terms of historical materialism on the world scale implies that we appreciate the worldwide character of commodities (and therefore of value) and the worldwide mobility of capital. These are only tendencies, of course, but they are essential tendencies, since they signify domination by capital on the scale of the system as a whole.

From working out this articulation of the globalized capitalist economy with the national and international social struggles and political conflicts, I have drawn the conclusion that the "North-South conflict" cannot be separated from the conflict between the tendency to reproduce specifically capitalist social relationships, on one side, versus the requirements for socialist transcendence of those relationships, on the other.

4. UNEQUAL ACCESS TO THE NATURAL RESOURCES OF THE PLANET

Classic vulgar economics took an interest in natural resources only insofar as they became the object of private appropriation. Such resources were then treated as "factors of production," as such entitling their owners to an income (a rent) determined by its productivity. Contrariwise, Marx analyzes these rents as categories of distribution, that is to say, as shares drawn from aggregate surplus-value. For him, natural resources create no value even though constituting an important foundation of social wealth.

Now that exploitation of the planet's resources has become quite inordinate, whether of those that can be objects of ownership (as, in general, subsoil resources) or of those that cannot (like the atmosphere), we are forced to revisit the question of how to deal with the "natural" conditions of production. Contemporary vulgar economics, nevertheless, remains fixed on its principles, seeking to "integrate" these new "factors of production" into its habitual line of argument in order to "price" them. For my part I go about it quite differently, and I will say so: by extending fearlessly the line of argument initiated by Marx. For the emergence of these questions, precisely, constitutes the finest evidence of the limits that so-called economic science cannot go beyond, and calls on us to deepen the radical critique of, on one side, capitalist reality and, on the other, of its alienated portrayals formulated by the new (so-called "green") vulgar economics, on the other.

The question of natural resources—those of the planet, of course—by its very nature puts the asymmetric globalized system of really existing capitalism/imperialism to the question. The strategies and practices implemented by the dominant centers are endeavors to retain, for their profit, exclusive access to those resources. By this fact imperialist rent takes on a second dimension, superimposed on that drawn from the globalized hierarchy of prices for labor-power.

In the following pages we will take up the totality of these problems, starting with"Mining Rent" (the historical starting point for dealing with the question of natural resources) in order to open up a broader discussion on unowned resources and to conclude by examining the major North-South conflicts over this decisive issue that puts the future of humanity at stake.

5. THEORY AND PRACTICE OF EXTRACTIVE RENT

Does the Marxist theory of ground rent apply to the sphere of *mining*? Here we have the same situation of need for access to natural conditions of production, and of capital sometimes finding itself up against a barrier constituted by property ownership. However, mining presents some obvious special features.

The first of these is the nonrenewability of the resources to be exploited. This feature imposes a specific cost of production that does not enter into rent, namely, the cost of replacement. Under the capitalist system, the operator, the mining capitalist, usually takes this cost into account. But then this factor is determined by the conditions of capitalism's functioning, which means that it is limited in two ways: (1) by the time prospect of the capitalists' calculation of profit, and (2) by the time prospect of the concession by virtue of which they are allowed access to the resource in question. These two limits are usually not independent of each other. Mining capitalists must therefore be sure to put aside an amount sufficient to enable them to continue their activities, at the same rate of profit, when the mines they are working become exhausted. Thus, the mining capitalists devote part of their apparent gross profit (actually, this part is a cost) to exploration for new reserves, both in the area conceded to them and elsewhere. The relatively brief time prospect of the operation reflects the well-known fact that reserves are proportionate to output, and not vice versa: generally speaking, at any moment in history, reserves seem to be sufficient to satisfy no more than a score of years of exploitation.

The cost of this exhaustion of resources for the community is quite different. I have already stated my view that mastery of social development by society itself implies a considerably longer time prospect than that of capitalist calculation, the rationality of which appears, in this respect, to be relative and short-term. When, for example, society grants a concession by an act of state, the problem presents itself like this: when the resource becomes exhausted, the amount set aside for replacement must be adequate to have enabled an investment to be made that is sufficient *either* for a new mine of the same product to be exploited at the same social cost, *or* to substitute for this natural product an artificial substitute of the same use-value and with the same cost, *or*, finally to replace this resource by another productive activity, in another domain (providing different use-values) but regarded as equivalent (that is, producing the same added value).

Some questions still remain open: (1) the uncertain character of such calculations (over a period of fifty years, for instance), an uncertainty that cannot be eliminated in any society, even a socialist one; (2) the problem of how, this being so, a classless society can technically rationalize its collective choices.

Is it necessary to add that this calculation goes beyond the question (which is insoluble anyway) of "external economies and diseconomies". These factors may be allowed for to some extent under capitalism, by means of legislation imposing compensatory taxes.

Is it necessary also to add that nonrenewability is less peculiar to mineral production than it may seem to be? Cultivable soil is not inexhaustible, either, unless it be properly maintained; and the historical experience of capitalism shows, in this case too, how limited is its rationality (the irreversible wastage of soils under capitalism, especially in the periphery, is a fact of history). But there is more to it than that: resources that appear to be inexhaustible (air and water) need—when a certain degree of intensity of industrialization has been reached—to be maintained in the same way as the soil, as has recently been discovered in connection with what is known as the problem of the environment.

The second specific feature of mineral production is of an historical order. Mineral production appears and develops with the development of capitalism, whereas agricultural production, of course, predated capitalism. Capitalist ground rent grafted itself onto a preexistent category, but extractive rent had practically no connection with any antecedent.

Apart from that fact, however, the sphere of mining presents no special features at this stage.

One observes, therefore, in this domain as in that of agriculture, the phenomenon of differential rents. To be sure, these rents find specific forms of expression in mining. The heavy technology employed in mining emphasizes rents of type II (connected with intensification of investment) rather than those of type I. The obstacle to entry into this sector that is constituted by the amount of capital needed causes the differential rents frequently to be combined with monopoly super-profits (in the vulgar sense of the expression) of the sort known as "technological" (which may or may not be temporary) that ought not to be confused, conceptually at least, with rent.

Absolute extractive rent sometimes makes its appearance over and above these costs, differential rents, and super-profits. It is at this level that, with respect to the conditions in which it is formed, determined, and spent, absolute extractive rent offers analogies with as well as specific differences from, ground rent.

Extractive rent, like ground rent, appears when a particular social class controls access to the resources in question. Whenever the owners of the soil also put to advantage their rights over the subsoil, they imposed an extractive rent on the capitalist operators. An example of this is the rent charged for the oilfields of the United States (meaning the absolute rent paid to the owners of the poorest deposits, not differential rents, which are indeed appropriated by those companies that exploit the richer deposits—for example, the ones in the Middle East). Generally, though, in the domain of mining, the capitalist state, acting in the name of the collective interests of the bourgeoisie, while asserting a right of ownership over the subsoil, was satisfied with allowing the dominant sectors of capital more or less free access to these resources in return for merely symbolic royalties.

The same applied on the plane of the world system. Control by the imperialist states over the colonies, and even over states enjoying formal independence, had for a long time the corollary of free access for the monopolies to the natural resources of the periphery, as is shown by the gratuitous concessions granted by the colonial administrations or wrested by means of gunboat diplomacy, or else obtained by paying a mere symbolic royalty, a "baksheesh" falling into the category of capital's overhead costs, rather than rent.

Extractive rent has emerged in recent times, on the plane of the world system, when the states of the periphery have begun trying to impose a real royalty for access to their resources.

At the conceptual level we must distinguish clearly between the *rentier* state and the capitalist firm exploiting the minerals, whether this be foreign or native, even if, in the latter case, it is a state-owned firm. Since the product in question is exported, the conditions of its exploitation, making possible a profit for the operating capital as well as a rent, are determined by the confrontation, on the world scale, between the state that owns the resources and the monopoly capital that dominates the mining activity.

These monopolies are, of course, no more in the position of farmers in agriculture than the states are in the position of landlords. The analogy has its obvious limitations. The superficial formulation of the neoclassicists would speak here of "bilateral monopoly," in contrast to the "pure and perfect" double competition of the farmers and landlords. I prefer to avoid this sort of formal analysis and to describe instead the classes engaged.

At this point we need to ask how the level of extractive rent is determined. Here again we cannot be satisfied with a "spectrum theory," which would state that this rent is situated between zero and the level at which it would absorb the whole of the world's surplus-value.

Vulgar economics is obsessed with the false concept of "true prices," whether for ordinary commodities, for labor, for money, for time, or for natural resources. There are no "true prices" to be "revealed" by the genius of the "market." Prices are the combined products of rates of exploitation of labor (rates of surplus-value), of competition among fragmented capitals and the deduction levied in the form of "oligopoly rents," and of the political and social conditions that govern the division of surplus-value among profits, interest, ground rents, and extractive rents.

Extractive rents are thus determined by the compromises resulting from confrontation between the owners of the subsoil, on

one side, and the capitalist class as a whole, on the other. And precisely because the deduction represented by extractive rent
involves the overall system of reproduction of capital, the intervention of the public powers has always, in this domain, been decisive.

6. ECOLOGY AND UNSUSTAINABLE DEVELOPMENT

1.

Our Ecological Footprint by Marthis Wackernagel and William
Rees (1996), investigated a major strand in radical social thinking
about construction of the future. The authors not only defined a
new concept—that of an ecological *footprint*—they also developed a *metric* for it, whose units are defined in terms of "global
hectares," comparing the biological capacity of societies/coun-
tries (their ability to produce and reproduce the conditions for
life on the planet) with their consumption of resources made
available to them by this bio-capacity.

The authors' conclusions are worrying. At the global level,
the bio-capacity of our planet is 2.1 global hectares (gha) per
capita (i.e., 13.2 billion gha for 6.3 billion inhabitants). In contrast, the global average for consumption of resources was
already—in the mid-1990s—2.7 gha. This "average" masks a
gigantic imbalance, the average for the triad (Europe,
North America, and Japan) having already reached a multiple on
the order of four magnitudes of the global average. A good proportion of the bio-capacity of societies in the South is taken up
by and to the advantage of these centers.

In other words, the current expansion of capitalism is destroying the planet and humanity.

This expansion's logical conclusion is either the actual geno-
cide of the peoples of the South—as "overpopulation"—or, at the
least, their confinement to ever-increasing poverty. An eco-fascist

strand of thought is being developed that gives legitimacy to this
type of "final solution" to the problem.

2.

The interest of this work goes beyond its conclusions. For it is a
question of a calculation (I use the term "calculation" rather than
"discourse"), deliberately put in terms of the use-value of the
planet's resources, illustrated through their measurement in
global hectares (gha), not in dollars.

The proof is therefore given that social use-value can be the
subject of perfectly rational calculation. This proof is decisive in
its import, since socialism is defined in terms of a society founded
on use-value and not on exchange-value. And defenders of capitalism have always held that socialism is an unreal utopia
because—according to them—use-value is not measurable,
unless it is conflated with exchange-value (defined in terms of
"utility" in vulgar economics).

Recognition of use-value (of which the measurement of economic footprints is but one good example) implies that socialism
should be "ecological," indeed can only be ecological, as Altvater
proclaims ("solar socialism" or "no socialism"). But it also implies
that this recognition is impossible in any capitalist system, even a
"reformed" one, as we shall see.

3.

In his time, Marx not only suspected the existence of this problem, he had already expressed it through his rigorous distinction
between use-value and wealth, conflated in vulgar economics.
Marx explicitly said that the accumulation of capital destroys the
natural bases on which that accumulation is built: man (the alien-

ated, exploited, dominated, and oppressed worker) and the earth (symbol of natural riches at the disposal of humanity). And whatever might be the limitations of this way of putting it, trapped within its own era, Marx's analysis nonetheless remains an illustration of a clear consciousness (beyond intuition) of the problem, which deserves to be recognized.

It is regrettable, therefore, that the ecologists of our time, including Wackernagel and Rees, have not read Marx. This would have allowed them to take their own proposals further, to grasp their revolutionary import, and, of course, to go further than Marx himself on this topic.

4.

This deficiency in modern ecology facilitates its capture by the ideology of vulgar economics, which occupies a dominant position in contemporary society. This capture is already under way and is, indeed, considerably advanced.

Political ecology (such as that proposed by Alain Lipietz) was located from the beginning within the gamut of the "pro-socialist," political left. Subsequently, "green" movements (and then political parties) located themselves in the center-left, through their expressed sympathy with social and international justice, their critique of "waste," and their concern with the fate of workers and "poor" peoples. But, apart from the diversity of these movements, we should note that none of them has established a rigorous relationship between the authentic socialist dimension necessary to the challenge and the no less necessary ecological dimension. To achieve this relationship, we should not ignore the wealth/value distinction emphasized by Marx.

The capture of ecology by vulgar ideology operates on two levels: on the one hand, by reducing measurement of use-value to an "improved" measure of exchange-value and, on the other, by integrating the ecological challenge with the ideology of "consensus." Both these maneuvers undermine the clear realization that ecology and capitalism are, by their nature, in opposition.

5.

This capture of ecological measurement by vulgar economics is making huge strides.

Thousands of young researchers in the United States, and their imitators in Europe, have been mobilized in this cause.

The "ecological costs" are, in this way of thinking, assimilated to external economies.

The vulgar method of measuring cost/benefit in terms of exchange-value (itself conflated with market price) is then used to define a "fair price," integrating external economies and diseconomies.

It goes without saying that the work—reduced to mathematical formulas—done in this traditional area of vulgar economics does not say how the "fair price" calculated could become that of the actual current market. It is presumed, therefore, that fiscal and other "incentives" could be sufficient to bring about this convergence. Any proof that such a convergence would really occur is entirely absent.

In fact, as can already be seen, oligopolies have seized hold of ecology to justify the opening up of new fields to their destructive expansion. Francois Houtart provides a conclusive illustration of this in his work on biofuels. Since then, "green capitalism" has been part of the obligatory discourse of those in positions of power, on both the right and the left, in the triad, and the CEOs of oligopolies. The ecology in question, of course, conforms to the vision known as "weak sustainability" (the notion that it is possible for the market to substitute for all natural resources, none of which is indispensable in defining a sustainable path)—

in other words, the complete commodification of the "rights of
access to the planet's resources." Joseph Stiglitz, in a report of the
UN commission that he chaired, openly embraced this position at
the United Nations General Assembly, June 24–26, 2009, pro-
posing "an auction of the world's resources (fishing rights,
licenses to pollute, etc.). This is a proposal that quite simply
comes down to sustaining the oligopolies in their ambition to
mortgage further the future of the peoples of the South.

6.

The capture of ecological discourse by the political culture of the
consensus (a necessary expression of the conception of capitalism
as the end of history) is equally well advanced.

This capture has an easy ride. For it is responding to the alienation and illusion that feed the dominant culture, that of capitalism. An easy ride because this culture is actual, and holds a dominant place in the minds of the majority of human beings, in the
South as well as the North.

In contrast, the expression of the demands of the socialist
counterculture is fraught with difficulty—because socialist culture is not there in front of our eyes. It is part of a future to
be invented, a project of civilization, open to the creativity of the
imagination. Formulae (such as "socialization through democracy and not through the market" and "the transfer of the decisive
level for decision-making from the economic and political levels
to that of culture") are not enough, despite their power to pave
the way for the historical process of transformation. For what is at
stake is a long, "secular" process of societal reconstruction, based
on principles other than those of capitalism, in both the North
and the South—a process that cannot be "rapid." But the construction of the future, however far away, begins today.

7. THE NORTH-SOUTH CONFLICT OVER ACCESS
TO THE PLANET'S RESOURCES

The question of "Mining Rent," or, more generally, of the income that countries can draw from natural resources situated within their territory, is inseparable from the forms in which imperialist capital imposes its domination over the subordinated periphery. The treatment of this question is hence closely linked to analysis of the phases of imperialism, the international class alliances that associate themselves with it, and the international division of labor that these govern. To each phase thus corresponds a certain simultaneous arrangement of production and demand, an adequate structuring of the distribution of income: grade scaling of prices for labor-power, level and rate of profit, quantity and rate of ground rents, and quantity of income derived from natural resources.

As a first approximation, we distinguish three phases in the evolution of capital accumulation within the imperialist system.

In the course of the first phase (the long nineteenth century up to the 1930s and 1960s, depending on which country or region) the international division of labor, of the colonial type, keeps the periphery confined to exportation of mineral and agricultural products. This division of labor, based on the class alliance between imperialism and the traditional local ruling classes, involves a structure of relative prices for commodities traded at the world level that favors accumulation of industrial capital at the center, permitting wage increases paralleling the development of the productive forces.

The price structures corresponding to this equilibrium offer a place to the ground rents remunerating the landed proprietor allies of imperialism, but have no place for mining rents—the capital of the imperialist monopolies reserving for itself free access to the periphery's subsoil resources and confining development of the bourgeoisie in the dominated regions to its comprador sector.

It is often forgotten that the easy growth of the "thirty glorious years" (1945–1975) was linked to a price for energy (in particular for petroleum) that had fallen to nearly nothing.

The second phase of modern asymmetric globalization begins with the victories of the national liberation movements of the Asian and African countries, "the Bandung era" (1955–1980), and the spread of the Nonaligned Movement. This second phase is characterized by import-substitution industrialization, imposing a renewal of international class alliances and substituting the national bourgeoisie for the former ruling classes.

During this phase, the dynamic equilibrium continues to work mainly on the basis of wage growth, accentuated by the maintenance of unequal exchange—the periphery continuing to provide primary materials under conditions of wage stagnation for labor, with which it pays thenceforward for importing industrial capital equipment instead of the consumption goods heretofore imported. Ground rents sometimes disappear when the feudal alliance is smashed by means of bourgeois agrarian reforms that establish new classes of *kulaks* and middle peasants. The ensuing relative reduction of farm prices serves the interests of the local bourgeoisie engaged in import substitution industrialization and also of imperialism, to the extent that those agricultural products continue to be exported toward the center.

Nevertheless, whatever the limits of this first moment of "the awakening of the global South," the movement of the peoples and nations of Bandung did not delay posing the question of the income to be gained by the countries concerned from their natural resources. Bandung proclaimed the principle of exercising national sovereignty over those resources and attained, although belatedly, in 1973, the imposition, as is known, of an upward revision of crude oil prices.

This "readjustment" in the conditions of access to natural resources (of which the crude-oil price is a symbol) was not of an "anti-capitalist" nature. The inclusion of rents (petroleum rents, as it happened) in the price of natural-resource products exported by the South would ameliorate the financial capabilities of the peripheral bourgeoisie and would allow it to embark upon a new stage of industrialization based, this time, on exportation of industrial products toward the centers. The delocalization of certain industries, abandoning the North, by reestablishing a reserve army of the unemployed would allow a simultaneous rising of the rate of profit. The expansion would then be initiated by the Southern export industries, on the basis of which new propulsive industries could resume their expansion in the North. This perspective—whose nature is entirely capitalist—of overcoming the contradictions of the world system constituted the program of the peripheral bourgeoisies at that time.

The imperialist triad rejected all propositions for a "new international economic order," even though the readjustment of crude-oil prices had finally to be accepted. Very diverse theses have been put forward on this subject. Some have accentuated the objective economic conditions of energy production: for example, the trend reversal in the relative cost of crude oil which, after a century of decreases, would have, starting in the 1960s, begun a long-term increasing trend. Others emphasize inter-imperialist contradictions and point to the will of the United States to reverse a situation that was turning against them (dollar crisis, etc.), by mobilizing the oil multinationals and the petroleum-producing states against Europe and Japan. Some even go further and view this collusion as a manifestation of the strategy of the multinationals, which would have chosen to ally themselves with the third-world states against the central states. The aim of the multinationals would have been, by delocalizing the industries under their control, to restore their rate of profit.

The "readjustments" in the Northern economies designed to "absorb the oil shock" did in fact inspire strategies that allowed capital to go back on the offensive and to dismantle the previous gains of their working classes (the postwar social-democratic compromise). These strategies succeeded in imposing on those working classes the structural adjustments needed to allow a restart of the stalled accumulation process.

So the "new order" project finally got under way (the de-localizations are its expression). But it was not under the control of the peripheral bourgeoisie and of their states—and to their profit—as had been envisaged in the original project. It was set in motion by, and to the profit of, the oligopoly capital of the imperialist centers. This operation opened the—short—era of so-called neoliberal globalization, which I have termed a second "*belle époque*."[4] The rapid and expected exhaustion of this phase of globalization has created the conditions for a "second wave of Southern awakening," beginning even before the financial collapse of 2008.

The ruling classes of the Southern states—or at least of those of them termed "emerging"—have regained the initiative and entered into accelerated industrialization and agricultural "modernization." Pursuit of their enterprise requires that these countries experience a surge in access to the planet's resources even while the cost of exploiting the better among those resources, increasingly rare, has become much higher than it had been. Beyond even these cost questions, the battle has now been contested on the field of access itself to these resources. The imperialist triad intends to keep it to itself—which is necessary to continue its "way of life" and is the basis for the social consensus that assures stability to the power of capital—by the brutal means of military control over the planet. By virtue of that fact, this North-South conflict has become the major conflict of our epoch.

The range of natural resources concerned is far wider than was envisaged even a short time ago. It involves crude oil and natural gas, but equally rare minerals, water, and agricultural land—access to which has been put at stake in conflicts over control and usage—and even the atmosphere (and, through it, the climate).

In these conditions it is impossible to settle the question of determination of extractive rent (or, more generally, the cost of access to the resources in question) in general terms. It must be made the object of concrete analyses of concrete situations. For every mineral, specific circumstances are the conditions for the struggle over its rent, and its possible outcomes. Thus, for a comparative example, one might cite iron ore, long produced only in the developed countries for their steel industries. As the needs of the central steel industries are no longer capable of being supplied by the former big producers, the West has secured itself a "mining belt" composed of secure countries (Canada, Brazil, South Africa, and Australia) that can supply ore at competitive prices in quantities sufficient for the foreseeable future. In these conditions the third-world producers (Venezuela, Mauritania, Guinea, India, Malaysia) are "marginalized" and deprived of negotiating leverage (especially if Brazil goes on refusing to support them). But, on the other side, considerable financial resources are needed to set up third-world steel industries. We see here a possible new association: OPEC countries, China, and the mineral-producing countries. Such an association would reinforce the collective autonomy of the Third World and would dissociate the ore/steel grouping of the periphery from that of the center, whose dominating effect at present is imposed alike over the ore-producing and steel-producing countries of the Third World. In an association of this sort, the "mining rent" would have to be negotiated on a state-to-state basis.

What use, in fact, is to be made of the rent by the countries that would be its beneficiaries obviously depends on the nature of the classes in a dominant position. In the most extreme case— one that is still common—this rent can be entirely wasted by the ruling cliques whose maintenance in power it guarantees, without the popular classes or even the country seeing hide nor hair of it (the rent not being invested in economic development). In other cases—the countries of the Persian Gulf—the rent quite simply goes to feed the globalized financial market controlled by the imperialist oligopolies. These ways of using the rent by stipendi-ary states or by powerless archaic regimes are, for dominant impe-rialism, quite acceptable. Contrariwise, when the rent is put to use for development, even capitalist development—as is the case in the emerging countries—conflict becomes inevitable.

8. HAS IMPERIALIST RENT BEEN CALLED INTO QUESTION?

The visible part of imperialist rent—that which arises from the grade scaling of labor-power prices—is already, in and of itself, gigantic and can be measured by anyone willing to take the trou-ble to do so. This part can be confiscated by the Southern coun-tries only to the extent that they disconnect themselves—if only relatively—by prioritizing in their development their internal market and the needs of their popular classes. Then, and only then, is the anti-imperialist posture articulated with the initiation of an overstepping of capitalist social relationships and enters on the long road to socialism.

The submerged part of the rent—access to the planet's resources—although not "measurable" (because that access lies outside the field of economics), is no less decisive. Here the battle turns on affirmation of the Southern countries' sovereignty over these resources, together with the commitment to prioritize internal development. Through this choice the Southern countries would reject submission to the perspective of "apartheid on a world scale" whose full extension would be imposed by imperialist logic.

Imperialist rent is quite equally and inseparably linked to the other monopolistic privileges of the imperialist countries, in par-ticular those involving access to technologies (firmly protected by the rules of the World Trade Organization), to communications, and to armaments of massive destruction. Politics here is indissol-ubly linked to economics, and vice versa.

Through entering on these paths, the Southern nations by their victories would create conditions in the North that would once again challenge the consensus founded on profits deriving from imperialist rent. The advance posts of the Northern peoples are dependent on defeat of the imperialist states in their confrontation with the Southern nations.

Concluding Political Remarks

I will conclude the analysis of the metamorphoses of value that I have projected in this work with a few reflections on their political significance.

1.

Capitalism cannot be reduced to its conceptualization as an "economic system," and still less to that—even more simplistic—of a "market economy." Behind the capital accumulation that governs it looms the active intervention of the market alienation that conditions its deployment. This market alienation is a complex concept, and cannot be reduced to the simplistic formula according to which "markets lay down the law." Alienation takes on multiple forms. It asserts itself across the appearance of capital, and becomes, alongside the other factors of production (labor, nature, science), a "factor of production" on its own. It asserts itself in the illusion that makes the worker who sells his labor-power believe that he is selling his labor. It asserts itself, to a more abstract degree, in the appearance that commodities are produced by commodities without the intervention of labor and that money is itself productive (that money "has babies"), or that time is "productive" ("time is money"). We have met up with each of these facets of capitalism's peculiar alienation at every stage in the analysis of the metamorphoses of value. We have seen that vulgar economics, because it ignores alienation, was by virtue of that fact unable to take full account of the significance of the extension of accumulation. Alienation is the backbone of the ruling class's ideology, becoming (as Gramsci said) the ruling ideology in society, and by that fact an active factor indispensable to the reproduction of the capitalist relations of production.

Equilibrium between supply and demand for the output of each of the two (intensively or extensively) expanding Departments has to be realized from one period to the next, whether that period be taken as short term (one year, for example) or as long-term, the time needed fully to depreciate invested capital equipment (ten years, for example) before its replacement. The expanded equilibrium equations—in values, or after their successive transformations into prices of production, into market prices, and into globalized prices—make it possible to identify the objective conditions necessary for the realization of that equilibrium (the distribution of investments and the labor force between the two Departments and the level of wages, which are functions of the growing productivity of social labor in each of the Departments). Knowledge—possible in such a case—of these conditions might be very useful in a prospective planning of economic reproduction. But capitalism by its nature is ignorant of planification, synonymous with social mastery over the economy. Its economic evolution ("growth") stems from decentralized decisions by the "deciders," the capitalists.

Defenders of the existing order (following Hayek) claim that this decentralized procedure is "efficacious" because it "reveals" the conditions of an equilibrium and, in the last analysis, offers assurance that it will be realized. Contrariwise, Marx proves that capitalism is naturally unstable. Decisions taken at a given moment, themselves occurring in a framework defined by the results of class struggles and interstate conflicts, commit the system to go from disequilibrium to disequilibrium without ever "tending objectively" toward equilibrium.

So bourgeois economic science (conventional vulgar economics), which tasks itself with discovering the conditions under which equilibrium can be realized, is looking for a "right" answer to a false and absurd question. For that reason I have compared it to the question of "the sex of the angels" which theologians of the Middle Ages sought to answer, thus helping themselves better to understand the imaginary world into which they had confined their thoughts. As they fled forward in search of conditions that would offer assurance of stability to a naturally unstable system, conventional economists were forced to invent a concept of "expectations;" the system thus being shaped in its evolution by the "expectations" of its economic actors. It is an immediately obvious and empty observation that enables them to envisage all possible and imaginable developments, and thus to foresee nothing at all. The system tends toward an imaginary equilibrium if expectations are of the sort that would lead it to do so. It would be hard to formulate a finer empty tautology.

Capitalism takes on its completed form only with the realization of its double revolution. On one side is the political revolution affirming the decisive political power of the bourgeoisie (in the successive forms of the, scarcely glorious, English "Glorious Revolution" of 1688, of the American War of Independence, and above all of the French Revolution, which is the starting point for modern politics). On the other the industrial revolution that initiates, with the spread of large-scale industry, its affirmed domination over economic life and the capitalist market alienation through which that domination is expressed. With fully formed capitalism the economic system becomes, for the first time in history, a generalized market system embracing

the products of social labor, labor-power, and the right to ownership of shares in capital. The expression "market economy" con-
ceals the reality of this system, which ought to be called an "economic system of capitalist markets." This form, through which is
expressed the reality of capitalist production relations, is historically novel.

2.

Capitalism is not at all what exists in the imagination of its high
priests. It is only a brief historical parenthesis but yet a decisive
parenthesis. Capitalism went through a long incubation—seven
to ten centuries prior to the French and industrial revolutions—
involving all the Afro-Eurasian societies, from China to the
Middle East to the cities of Italy, until it finally coagulated into its
historic form as European capitalism. The flowering of the capitalist world, its "Schumpeterian" inventive and creative moment,
was short, less than a century from the French and industrial revolutions to the Paris Commune of 1871.

Capitalism then enters on its first long crisis, from 1873 (so
say the economists—I would say from 1871, the date of the
Commune) to 1945. A very long crisis indeed, that Lenin, opti-
mistically, thought would be the last. A crisis whose second
part—from 1914 to 1945—saw successively the First World War,
the Russian Revolution, the 1929 crisis, the rise of Nazism and
imperial Japan, the Second World War, the Chinese revolution,
and the Vietnamese revolution which initiated the liberation of
Asia and Africa. These "events," which can hardly be qualified
as "minor," constituted the "response to that first crisis."

The second long crisis, which started with the U.S. termina-
tion of the international convertibility of the dollar to gold in
1971, has followed a path like that of the first part of the previous
crises: concentration of capitals, forced and violent globalization,

and financialization. It is now entering into its second part, whose outcome will be shaped by ever-intensifying interstate conflicts (in particular North versus South) and social struggles. I refer here to my own work, which suggests viewing these two crises as parallels.[1] Beyond analogies, it accentuated the qualitative transformations of the system from one crisis to the other, in particular the emergence of the collective imperialism of the triad (the United States, Europe, and Japan).

My reading of the history of capitalism meshes with the conclusions that Baran, Sweezy, Magdoff (and, following them, the *Monthly Review* team) have drawn from their precocious analysis of monopoly capitalism. Those conclusions are:

1. Capitalism is, by nature, a system that tends to produce a surplus that cannot be invested in the broadening and deepening of the productive system.

2.. Economic growth is therefore an exception whose (always peculiar) causes have to be discovered in each instance— not the rule and effect of the "fundamental rationality" of this system, which would by the same token be "without alternative" and synonymous with "the end of history."

3. The history of the nineteenth century is that of the installation of finished capitalism, spreading in a framework in which competitive practices still prevail over monopolistic ones: and that those conditions are at the origin of the success of rapid growth in the central economies' system, up to the moment when, with the full extension of its own capital-centralizing logic, the monopolies abolish the former system of competitive capitalism.

4. Since the end of the nineteenth century, with the first monopoly capitalism, the tendency to stagnate displays its

tenacious effects, which are overcome only through the parasitic growth of the surplus-absorbing "Department III."

5. Although the first long crisis did not conclude with the disappearance of capitalism, it nonetheless remains true that the prodigious growth of the "thirty glorious years" (1945–1975) was brief and finds its explanation in special conditions produced by the Second World War.

6. The tendency to stagnate, which came back to the surface with the inception in the 1970s of the second long crisis of monopoly capitalism, is partly overcome by financialization. The latter is not a "deviation" that might be corrected by appropriate forms of regulation; it is inseparable from the survival requirements of the system.

I have extended those analyses initiated by Baran, Sweezy, and Magdoff in the following four domains:

1. The recognition of the two successive moments of monopoly capitalism's extension, linked to its two long crises (1873–1945; 1971 to and beyond the present), and the identification of the new forms through which are expressed the deepening of the crisis of the system. This has become in our day the "late capitalism of generalized, financialized, and globalized oligopolies."

2. The analysis of the similar ways in which the monopolies have responded to the challenges posed by each of those two successive crises: concentration of capitals, financialization, and deepened globalization. Those responses assured the success of brief, though dazzling, "belle époque" moments of recovery (successively 1895–1914, then 1991–2008).

3. The passage from the conflict of national imperialisms (permanent until 1945) to the triad's collective imperialism.

4. The recognition of the decisive confrontation, opposing the imperialist triad to the awakening of the Southern nations, which showed itself at the outset through the first wave of revolutions carried out in the name of socialism (from semi-peripheral Russia to the peripheral countries China, Vietnam, and Cuba) and the spread of the Bandung projects (1955–1985). The transformation of the law of value into the law of globalized value gives an account of the nature of the challenge, of the contradictions and limitations in that first wave of attempts to escape from capitalism.

It thus becomes quite plain that an adequate "response to the current crisis" will not be given by the adoption of "effective economic policies" devised by technocrats in the service of capital, nor even by authentically reformist projects proposed by well-meaning leftists.

3.

As I have noted, I did not find satisfying answers in Marx to the question of the globalization of capitalism. I have sought to take up the challenge through recognition of the extraordinary fact that really existing capitalism, in its globalized extension, has produced, reproduced, and unceasingly deepened the centers–peripheries polarization.

I have dared to state that this extraordinary fact governs all struggles and political and social conflicts, at every national scale and at the global scale. I mean by this that both the social struggles of the classes exploited by capital against the exploiting classes (which take many and diverse forms) and the conflicts among the established powers in the centers and the peripheries are intertwined and mutually condition each other. Reduction of this reality, inseparable from the polarization stemming from the global expansion of capitalism, to a simple affirmation of determination "in the last analysis" by the class struggle pitting labor against capital excludes the difficult questions, the true questions, from the field of discussion. Its symmetrical reduction to power struggles, like geopolitical analysis of national policies, is no more worthwhile.

The difficult question involves the struggles of peoples (in the sense of the popular classes), of nations (in the sense of historical realities that have each developed their peculiar personality), and of states (in the sense of powers wielded in the name of these nations by the established ruling classes).

Do they offer the perspective that possibly capitalism can be "patched up" within its bounds and by capitalist methods? Were that possible, no force, no ideology, no cultural project would be capable of seriously hindering its advance. In that case, the "stages of growth" thesis would at last find itself confirmed—certainly not by virtue of the tranquil progression of "globalization" but through the incessantly renewed combat against its forms, from which stems the center–periphery asymmetry. In other words, the anti-imperialist dimension of those struggles would imply no rejection of the capitalist solution but rather the contrary, which is to say the adhesion within capitalism that the nations in question would have sought to impose, and would have succeeded in imposing, on the imperialist powers.

Or these struggles do not open the royal road of a "patch-up" within the system.

Recognition of the globalization of the law of value lets us understand why such a "patch–up" within the system is objectively impossible. From that fact it follows that anti-imperialist struggles are entangled in the struggle for a "different social system" (in the last analysis, for a socialist perspective). This intermeshing is reflected in the competition for "leadership" of the political anti-imperialist fronts between, on the one hand, the established class powers who "naturally" aspire to flourish in the form of national bourgeoisies forcing acceptance of their equal participation in shaping the future of the world and, on the other, the complex and alternative historical blocs centered, to diverse degrees, on the popular classes in the diversity of their expressions.

4.

For the second time in contemporary history the imperialist dimension of capitalism is being challenged. The first time was after the Second World War.

Since 1945, the United States of America, the dominant imperialist power of this epoch, has proclaimed the division of the world into two spheres, that of the "Free World" and that of "Communist Totalitarianism." The reality of the Third World was flagrantly ignored: it was felt to be privileged in belonging to the "free world," as it was "non-communist." "Freedom" was considered as applying only to capital, with complete disregard for the realities of colonial and semi-colonial oppression. The following year Zhdanov, in his famous report (in fact, Stalin's), which led to the setting up of the Cominform (an attenuated form of the Third International), also divided the world into two, the socialist sphere (the USSR and Eastern Europe) and the capitalist one (the rest of the world). The report ignored the contradictions within the capitalist sphere that opposed the imperialist centers to the peoples and nations of the peripheries who were engaged in struggles for their liberation.

The Zhdanov doctrine pursued one main aim: to impose peaceful coexistence and hence to calm the aggressive passions of the United States and its subaltern European and Japanese allies. In exchange, the Soviet Union would accept a low profile, abstaining from interfering in colonial matters that the imperialist powers considered their internal affairs. The liberation movements, including the Chinese revolution, were not supported with any enthusiasm at that time and they carried on by themselves. But their victory (particularly that of China, of course) was to bring about some changes in international power relationships.

Moscow did not perceive this until Bandung, which enabled it, through its support for the countries in conflict with imperialism, to break out of its isolation and become a major actor in world affairs. In a way, it is not wrong to say that the main change in the world system was the result of this first "Awakening of the South." Without this knowledge, the later affirmation of the new "emerging" powers cannot be understood.

The Zhdanov report was accepted without reservation in the European communist parties and in those of Latin America of that era. However, almost immediately it came up against resistance from the communist parties of Asia and the Middle East. This was concealed in the language of that period, for they continued to affirm "the unity of the socialist camp" behind the USSR, but as time went on resistance became more overt with the development of their struggles for regaining independence, particularly after the victory of the Chinese revolution in 1949. To my knowledge no one has ever written a history of the formulation of the alternative theory, which gave full rein to the independent initiatives of the countries of Asia and Africa, later to crystallize at Bandung in 1955 and then in the constitution of the Non-Aligned Movement (from 1960 defined as Asian-African, plus Cuba). The details are buried in the archives of some communist parties (those of China, India, Indonesia, Egypt, Iraq, Iran, and perhaps a few others).

Nevertheless, I can bear personal witness to what happened, having been lucky enough, since 1950, to have participated in one of the groups of reflection that brought together the Egyptian, Iraqi, and Iranian communists and some others. Information about the Chinese debate, inspired by Zhou Enlai, was not made known to us by Comrade Wang (the link with the journal *Révolution*, whose editorial committee included myself) until much later, in 1963. We heard echoes of the Indian debate and the split that it had provoked, which was confirmed afterwards by the constitution of the Communist Party of India (Marxist). We knew that debates within the Indonesian and Filipino communist parties had developed along the same lines.

This history should be written, as it would help people to understand that Bandung did not originate in the heads of the nationalist leaders (Nehru and Sukarno particularly, Nasser rather less) as is implied by contemporary writers. It was the product of a radical leftwing critique that was at that time conducted within the communist parties. The common conclusion of these groups of reflection could be summed up in one sentence: the fight against imperialism brings together, at the world level, the social and political forces whose victories are decisive in opening up possible socialist advances in the contemporary world.

That conclusion, however, left open a crucial question: who was to direct these anti-imperialist battles? To simplify: the bourgeoisie (then called "national"), whom the communists should then support, or a front of popular classes, directed by the communists and not the bourgeoisie (who were anti-national in fact)? The answer to this question often changed and was sometimes confused. In 1945 the communist parties concerned were aligned, based on the conclusion that Stalin had formulated: the bourgeoisie everywhere in the world (in Europe, aligned with the United States, as in the colonial and semi-colonial countries) has "thrown the national flag into the rubbish bin." The communists were therefore the only ones who could assemble a united front of the forces that refused to submit to the imperialist, capitalist, American order.

Mao reached the same conclusion in 1942, but it was only made known to us when his *New Democracy* had been translated into Western languages in 1952. This thesis held that, for the majority of the peoples of the planet, the long road to socialism could only be opened by a "national, popular, democratic, anti-feudal and anti-imperialist revolution run by the communists." The underlying message was that other socialist advances were not on the agenda elsewhere, i.e., in the imperialist centers. They could not possibly take shape until after the peoples of the peripheries had inflicted substantial damage on imperialism.

The triumph of the Chinese revolution confirmed this conclusion. The communist parties of Southeast Asia, in Thailand, Malaysia, and the Philippines in particular, started liberation struggles inspired by the Vietnamese model. Later, in 1964, Che Guevara revealed similar views when he called for "one, two, many Vietnams."

The vanguard proposals for initiatives by the independent and anti-imperialist countries of Asia and Africa, which were formulated by the different communist groups of reflection, were precise and advanced. They are to be found in the Bandung program and that of the Non-Aligned Movement, of which I gave a systematic presentation in my *L'eveil du Sud* (*Awakening of the South*). The proposals focused on the essential need to reconquer control over the accumulation process (through development that is auto-centered and delinked from the world economy).

It so happens that some of these proposals were adopted, although with considerable dilutions in certain countries, from 1955 to 1960, by the governing classes as a whole in both continents. And at the same time the revolutionary struggles waged by all the communist parties of Southeast Asia were defeated (except in Vietnam, of course). The conclusion would seem to be that the "national bourgeoisie" had not exhausted its capacity for anti-imperialist struggle. The Soviet Union also came to that conclusion when it decided to support the non-aligned front, while the imperialist triad declared open warfare against it.

The communists in the countries concerned were then divided between the two tendencies and became involved in

painful conflicts that were often confused. Some drew the lesson
that it was necessary to "support" the established powers that
were battling imperialism, although this support should remain
"critical." Moscow gave wind to their sails by inventing the thesis
of the "non-capitalist way." Others conserved the essentials of the
Maoist thesis, according to which only a front of the popular
classes that was independent of the bourgeoisie could lead a suc-
cessful struggle against imperialism. The conflict between the
Chinese communist party and the Soviet Union, which was apparent in 1957 but officially declared in 1960, of course confirmed the
second tendency among the Asian and African communists.

However, the potential of the Bandung movement wore out
within some fifteen years, emphasizing—if it should be needed—
the limits of the anti-imperialist programs of the "national bourgeoisies." Thus the conditions were ripe for the imperialist counter-
offensive, the "recompradorization" of the Southern economies, if
not—for the most vulnerable—their recolonization.

Nevertheless, as if to give the lie to the thesis of the definitive and
absolute impotence of the national bourgeoisies—Bandung having
been, according to this vision, just a "passing episode" in the Cold War
context—certain countries of the South have been able to impose
themselves as "emerging" in the new globalization dominated by
imperialism. But "emerging" in what way? Emerging markets open to
the expansion of capital of the oligopolies belonging to the imperialist
triad? Or emerging nations capable of imposing a genuine revision of
the terms of globalization and reducing the power exercised by the oligopolies, while redirecting accumulation to their own national development? The question of the social control of the established powers
in the emerging countries (and in other countries of the periphery)
and the prospects that this opens up or closes is once again on the
agenda. It is a debate that cannot be avoided: what will—or could—
be the nature of the "post crisis" world?

The crisis of the late imperialist countries of generalized,
financialized, and globalized oligopolies is patent. But even before

it passed into the new phase inaugurated by the financial collapse of 2008, people had begun to bestir themselves out of the lethargy that had set in after the first wave of struggles for the emancipation of workers and peoples had worn itself out.

Latin America, which had been absent during the Bandung era (in spite of Cuba's efforts with the Tricontinental), this time seemed even to be in advance of the rest of the movement.

There are of course many important new aspects in the present situation, but the same questions that were being posed in the 1950s are once again on the table. Will the South (emerging countries and others) be capable of taking independent strategic initiatives? Will popular forces be capable of imposing the kind of transformations in the power systems that are necessary for making serious progress? Can bridges be built that associate the anti-imperialist and popular struggles in the South with the progress of a socialist consciousness in the North?

I will refrain from giving quick answers to these difficult questions that only the development of struggles will resolve. But the importance of these discussions, in which the radical intellectuals of our era should commit themselves, must not be underestimated, nor the proposals that might result from such discussions.

The conclusions reached by the groups of reflection of the 1950s formulated the challenge in terms that have remained essentially the same ever since: the peoples of the periphery must undertake national construction (supported by regional plans and those of the South as a whole that are auto-centered and delinked); they cannot take this route unless their struggles are carried out in a socialist perspective; and for this reason they must shed their illusions about the false alternative of "catching up" to the globalized capitalist system. Bandung embodied this independent option but within certain limits, as history revealed.

Could the results be better now, when a second "Awakening of the South" is on the horizon? Above all, will it be possible this time to build convergences between the struggles in the North and in the South? These were lamentably lacking in the Bandung epoch. The peoples of the imperialist centers then aligned behind their imperialist leaders. The social-democratic project of the time would in fact have been difficult to imagine without the imperialist rent that benefited the opulent societies of the North. Bandung and the Non-Aligned Movement were thus seen as just an episode in the Cold War, perhaps even manipulated by Moscow. In the North, there was little understanding of the real dimensions of this first emancipatory wave of the countries of Asia and Africa which, however, was convincing enough for Moscow to give it support.

The challenge of constructing an anti-imperialist internationalism of workers and peoples remains to be tackled.

5.

Socialism (or better, communism) represents a more advanced stage of human civilization, which became conceivable with Marx's initiation of the fundamental critique of capitalism. Given that the invention of the capitalist stage of civilization stumbled for centuries before finding the particular form that assured its triumph, why then reject the idea that the invention of socialism should itself, likewise, be the product of successive waves? In that spirit, I have suggested a reading of the twentieth century— of the revolutions (Russian and Chinese) and of the first instances of Southern awakening (the nations of Africa and Asia)—as a first wave of the affirmation of the objective necessity of socialism, which is the sole alternative to the descent into barbarism implicit in the ongoing extension of historical (and imperialist by its nature) capitalism.

The growing contrast between the dominant center (profiting from imperialist rent) and the dominated peripheries of the historical capitalist system is the origin of the tragedy of the first-wave revolutions—those of the twentieth century—in the face of conflicting objectives: on one side, to develop the productive forces whose course had been diverted and whose progress was handicapped by imperialist domination and, on the other, to advance in constructing post capitalist social relationships on the long road leading to socialism. Once again, the transformation of the world is being initiated in the periphery of the established system.

Adhesion to the thought of a shoreless Marx does not equip one with a "crystal ball" that provides infallible foresight. No more does that adhesion furnish us with a "correct theory" allowing one to put forth infallible and efficacious strategies (we have seen a fine example in the twists and turns of the evaluations by communists regarding the Bandung project). It merely offers analytic tools superior to all others. Marx has taught us that the paths of history are set by the results of struggles and conflicts; history is not to be written before history itself has happened. Marx has likewise taught us that the solution to the most violent contradictions is to be found either in going beyond a social system that has become obsolete or else in the self-destruction of society. Today more than ever the terms of the alternative are clear: socialism or barbarism. Today more than ever capitalism's appearance conforms to its reality: a parenthesis in history, the continuance of whose extension can lead only to death.

There are good reasons to think that the nations of Asia, Africa, and Latin America (a minority comprising 80 percent of the human race!) will carry it off and will arrive, across what I call the "second wave of Southern awakening," at putting an end to imperialist rent. There are likewise good reasons to think that the Northern peoples—who are not "by nature" wicked devils— once deprived of the advantages of that rent which until now made them accept the terms of a "consenting" pro-imperialist allegiance, will be capable of forming themselves into alternative historic blocs open to the socialist perspective. The monopoly of power by the plutocracy that governs them, albeit reinforced, is not necessarily stable.

Undoubtedly, skeptics will tell us that we are far from having entered on those paths. The constitution of anti-plutocratic/anti-imperialist fronts is not to be seen taking form in the North. No more does one see political forces expressing the interests of the popular classes becoming capable, today, of "overturning" the established powers in the South. Overall, movements of protest and of struggle are still, in the North as in the South, fragmented and defensive. Accordingly, the initiative is still broadly in the sole hands of the established powers, which alone hold the forestage in the North as in the South. But optimism of the will, as Gramsci said, is based on the possibility of going beyond these preliminary stages of the confrontation—indeed, to going forward on the long transition to socialism, "There Is No Alternative."

It will force the peoples of the periphery to learn how to correctly link market and plan. In having recourse—quite inescapably—to the requirements of managing economic development by means of the market, they must keep in mind that in our epoch the "market" is still a "capitalist market" that promotes capitalist social relations and their accompanying alienations. Planification is the only way to lessen the danger of going fatally astray. This planification must not be envisaged as the bureaucratic management of a "state socialism" (in reality a state capitalism "without capitalists," pending its becoming capitalism with capitalists). This planification rest on forms still to be invented and on the active participation by the popular classes in all processes of decision making and methods of management, from the enterprise and from the village up to the nation. In this perspective, market and plan together combine methods at once complementary and conflicting.

This combination will be just as requisite in the developed capitalist societies, whose transformation likewise is not to be conceived as "rapid." Although the methods applied there to this combination will necessarily be different, since the issue is reconversion rather than development, the fundamental principles guiding the invention of the progression of socialization by means of democracy are identical.

Capitalism, far from settling in as the "end of history," constitutes but a brief parenthesis in history. It has realized, in a historically short span, a development of the productive forces broadly sufficient to make realistic as well as conceivable the socialist project of a higher stage of civilization. There is no "escape from the crisis" of capitalism; escape from capitalism, however, is visibly and objectively possible and necessary.

Initiation of the exit from capitalism and entering on the long road to socialism requires, at the outset, the elimination of private property by means of nationalizing the oligopolies—starting with this, the progressive invention of adequate ways to socialize their management becomes conceivable. Reforms not rising to the level of these requirements will remain unable to reduce the destructive power of capitalist management of the oligopolies.

As long as the peoples and nations of the peripheries remain unable to eliminate imperialist rent, or to substantially reduce it, there is small chance that public opinion in the opulent Northern societies will arrive at conceiving the inescapable necessity of nationalizing the oligopolies. Without any pertinence is the argument that the productive forces are still not sufficiently developed to allow for the abolition of capitalist social relationships. The Paris Commune (1871) already disproved that. The "technical" means needed to resolve the material problems of the whole human race already exist. But the logic of capitalism forbids setting them to their needed work. And the conditions of a "global consensus" that would allow this are not in place, as is proven by the recent Copenhagen Conference on climate change. Thus the fact remains that unequal capitalist development on the world scale (that is to say, pauperization of the peripheries) renders inescapable a development of the productive forces oriented in a direction, not of an imitative catch-up, but in a direction allowing for correction of the distortions stemming from imperialist domination of the global system.

Afterword

In the introduction to this work, I recalled that my reading of *Das Kapital* had aroused my enthusiasm yet had given me no greater understanding about the origin of Asian and African "underdevelopment." And I noted that all my subsequent analytical work—during a half-century—has gone into an effort to fill that lacuna.

In my view, Marx's opus remained unfinished. I am certainly not alone in recognizing this. Marx himself, in a letter to Lassalle, wrote: "the whole is divided into six books: 1) Capital, 2) Landed Property, 3) Wage Labor, 4) The State, 5) International Trade, 6) The World Market."[1]

As is well known, Marx published only the first volume of *Das Kapital* in his lifetime. Engels published the (nearly completed) manuscripts of Volumes II and III (parts of which deal with landed property and wage labor) posthumously; and Kautsky later published Marx's notes for Volume IV, which covers the history of theories of surplus value. The contemplated volumes dealing with the state and the system of globalized capitalism were never written.

I am interpreting the "silences" of that unfinished work, *Das Kapital*. I am indebted to Michael Lebowitz, author of *Following*

Marx, for this expression.[2] *Das Kapital*—and here Lebowitz and perhaps several others, like the Englishman E. P. Thompson, share my view—dissects (or "deconstructs") the logic of capital and adduces a critique of political economy (the subtitle of *Das Kapital*). The term "critique" must be understood not as the substitution of a "good" for a "bad" (or, at best, imperfect) economics but as specifying the status of political economy (in the loftiest sense of the term) as the foundation of bourgeois ideology.

This dissection allows Marx to make visible what is concealed in political economy: value and surplus-value, which show up in political economy only in the forms of price and profit. This operation is basic. Without it capitalism cannot be grasped in its reality and so would appear as a "rational" system of organizing production.

Marx thus envisaged completing this side of the analysis of capital with a book on wage-labor (the third book mentioned in the letter to Lassalle). Here Marx envisaged introducing the new class struggle (that of the wage-earning proletariat against the capitalist bourgeoisie) into the construction not of a "political economy" but of a "historical materialism" or "materialist history" (and I do mean materialist, plainly not "economic-determinist"). After all, wage labor is not a "fact of nature," and human beings try to escape from it whenever possible. As Marx points out in discussing the "new colonization" (the settler colonization of North America): the "natural" reproduction of the wage-labor force clashes with the handicap formed by its flight and establishment as independent farmers on conquered territory. Emancipation of those who, under capitalism, are wage laborers subordinate to capital (and exploited by it) comes through the abolition of wage labor (communism), not through its "humane management." The fragments of an analysis of wage labor published in the volumes of *Das Kapital* (supplemented with writings by Marx and Engels from newspaper articles and from their correspondence) clearly point to that intention. But they are no more than an indication; this "silence" would thus probably have been corrected in the third book that never appeared.

Pretty much the same can be said about the second book on "landed property." Capitalism was not produced by "reason's theoretical invention," as the Enlightenment thinkers imagined. Capitalism was built—gradually, then imposed as dominant—through the social struggles of the emerging bourgeoisie against the Old Regime, in concrete historical conditions of time and place, themselves differing from country to country. I have always maintained that the same sort of contradictions were at work elsewhere, from China to the Islamic Middle East. I refer here to my contribution to discussions on "global history" and "globalizations," to my book *Class and Nation*, and to my early criticism of Eurocentrism. But that discussion is only indirectly at issue here. Landed property, as discussed by Marx, is characterized by the transformation of feudal property (with superimposed rights of lords and—serf or free—peasant tenants) into purely capitalist agricultural property. Marx concentrates on that transformation, which he analyzes in some detail in his published writings (*Das Kapital* and other writings). What Marx inferred from this, in regard to ground rent, is discussed by me in this work and is further developed, even "corrected."

But it is only in the *Formen* (*Forms*) that Marx takes up the same question for other—"Asiatic"—societies. This work on precapitalist forms of production—one of Marx's 1857–1858 manuscripts—was only published belatedly (as a complement to the manuscript on principles for a critique of political economy) by Maximilien Rubel.[3] I have rejected those propositions, which indeed Marx neither published nor expanded later. The second book, if it had been written, would perhaps have thrown more light on the subject, but nobody can really know.

Although the fourth book, concerning the state, was also never written, the thought of Marx on this subject can be better understood than on the others. The bourgeois state is a concentrated expression of its economic reality, as Lenin expressed it. By that I mean not that it is solely "capital's state" ("in the service of capital") but that it is also the manager of the "whole," able if necessary to go against a multiplicity of capitalist interests in dealing with the wage-labor force. Still, it's likely that if Marx had written that fourth book he would have told us more on the subject, going beyond his concrete analyses of concrete situations—in particular those involving the nineteenth century political history of France from the 1848 revolution to the Commune. I have put forth several propositions involving a possible theory of the (class) state in societies before capitalism (those which I have termed "tributary"), accentuating the reversal of the relationship between politics and economics accompanying the substitution of the bourgeois state for the tributary state.[4]

My work mainly has bearing on the fifth and sixth of the books promised in his letter to Lassalle. These two books appear to split a single question into two parts: first in terms of "international trade"—the fifth book—and then in terms of the "world market"—the sixth book. At first sight, this is a strange way of going about it. Nevertheless, I have followed in Marx's footsteps on this question. I first (1973) offered a contribution to the discussions about "unequal exchange" in which I specified that this sort of exchange is a relationship between "countries" in which the range of prices for labor-power (real wages) shows a much wider range than that of the productivities of social labor (in the Marxian sense, which is quite different from what bourgeois economists call the "factor-productivity of labor"). Unequal exchange ("North-South," to put it simply) makes up only the visible part of the iceberg. The concept of "imperialist rent," central to the construction of what I call the law of globalized value, implies a deconstruction of everything constituting "globalized capitalist economics." Marx would perhaps have been led to advance some propositions on this subject if he had written that sixth book on "the world market." But obviously we will never know.

So then, could the present work be termed the "sixth book of *Capital*"? If by that we were to understand an "imaginative" exercise bearing on what Marx might have been able to write on the subject, the answer would be no. I have not undertaken in this work an exegesis of Marx's scattered passages dealing with "the world market" (the globalized capitalist system) in order to construct a sixth book as close as possible to what Marx might have written. I have no idea whether he would have discovered the dynamic of polarization or if, on the contrary, he would have emphasized a homogenizing tendency of the globalization process. I put forward, taking off from my analyses of the development of capitalist globalization, an abstract formalization of the globalized law of value which extends that of the law of value. Thus, in other terms, I am, in writing this sort of "sixth book" of *Capital*, deliberately placing myself in the contemporary world, not in that of 1875.

It is for the reader to judge whether this Marxist theory of the world capitalist system and of the law of globalized value is roadworthy, correctly extends the works of Marx, and respects their spirit. In any case, I hope that this publication will give rise to a discussion on the matter.

Notes

CHAPTER ONE: THE FUNDAMENTAL STATUS OF THE LAW OF VALUE

1. On the discussion over "markets" see V. I. Lenin, *Economic Romanticism*. *On the Market Question*; Rosa Luxemburg, *The Accumulation of Capital* (London: Routledge, 2003)(complete bibliography of the discussion as of that time); Mikhail Tugan-Baranovsky, *The Industrial Crises in England* (first German edition, 1901). My contribution to this discussion is expressed in *Le développement inégal* ["Uneven Development"], 146 ff.

2. E. H. Chamberlin, *The Theory of Monopolistic Competition* (Cambridge, MA: Harvard University Press, 1933); E. H. Chamberlin, *The Theory of Monopolistic Competition*, Boston, 1931; Joan Robinson, *The Economics of Imperfect Competition* (London: Macmillan, 1933); *Imperfect Competition* (London, 1935); Paul Baran and Paul Sweezy, *Monopoly Capital: An Essay on the American Economic and Social Order* (New York: Monthly Review Press, 1966). Baran and Sweezy, *Monopoly Capital*, 1936.

3. Samir Amin, *Au delà du capitalisme sénile* ["Beyond senile capitalism"], (Paris, 2002), 63 ff.

4. *Le développement inégal*, 74–76.

5. Ibid., to be found by the reader in *Le développement inégal* (pp. 66–98).

6. Samir Amin, *Itineraire intellectuel*, 187; *La crise*, 10–12.

7. Samir Amin, *Les défis de la mondialization* ["Challenges of globalization"], ch. IV; *L'avenir de la polarization mondiale* ["The future of global polarization"].

8. *Au delà du capitalisme sénile.*

9. My interventions in these discussions, like the propositions that I have put forward in response to the challenges, are summarized in *Du capitalisme à la civilization* ["From capitalism to civilization"], 84–95.

10. On the reduction of progress to GDP growth see my *Du capitalisme à la*

civilization, ch. 3, 98 ff.; on the likening of progress to emancipation see my *Modernité, Religion, et Démocratie* ["Modernity, Religion, and Democracy"], introductory chapter.

11. *Du capitalisme à la civiliization,* 77–84.
12. Samir Amin, *Critique de l'air du Temps* ["Critique of the climate of opinion"], ch. V, 66–80.

CHAPTER TWO: INTEREST, MONEY, AND THE STATE

1. Samir Amin, *Le développement inégal,* 66–98.
2. Samir Amin, *Unequal Development* (New York: Monthly Review Press, 1976), 104–32.
3. *Le développement inégal,* 88–112.
4. On this plane, the analyses of S. de Brunhoff, though they stay too close to mere exegesis of Marx where the supply of money is concerned, have very properly reminded us of the close relation between the state and money that is intrinsic to the analysis given in *Capital.*

CHAPTER THREE: GROUND RENT

1. Henri Regnault, *La contradiction foncière* ["The agrarian contradiction"], thesis, Paris, 1975.
2. Samir Amin, *Imperialism and Unequal Development* (New York: Monthly Review Press, 1977), ch. 2.
3. See the history of this development as given by Claude Faure, *Agriculture et mode de production capitaliste* (Paris: Anthropos, 1978).
4. Samir Amin and Kostas Vergopoulos, *La question paysanne et le capitalisme* ["The peasant question and capitalism"] (Paris: Anthropos, 1974); *Imperialisme et développement inégal* (1976); *Le capitalisme et la rente foncière* ["Capitalism and ground rent"], 45–82; Samir Amin et al., *Les luttes paysannes et ouvrières face aux défis du XXIième siècle* ["Peasant and worker struggles confronting the challenges of the 21st century"] (Les Indes Savants, 2005).

CHAPTER FOUR: ACCUMULATION ON A GLOBAL SCALE

1. Samir Amin, *La déconnexion* ["The disconnection"] (1986), 233–297.
2. Samir Amin, *Unequal Development* (New York: Monthly Review Press, 1976), 104–32.
3. Samir Amin, *Le développement inégal,* 60–65 and 164–169.
4. Samir Amin, *Au delà du capitalisme sénile,* 11ff.

CONCLUDING POLITICAL REMARKS

1. Samir Amin, *La crise. Sortir de la crise du capitalisme ou sortir du capitalism en crise* ["The crisis. To escape from the crisis of capitalism or to escape from capitalism in crisis"] (2009).

NOTES   139

AFTERWORD
1. Marx to Ferdinand Lassalle, February 22, 1858, http://www.marxistsfr
    .org/archive/marx/works/1858/letters/58_02_22.htm.
2. Michael Lebowitz, *Following Marx: Method, Critique and Crisis* (Leiden:
    Brill, 2009).
3. Marx's Formen is available in English in Eric Hobsbawm, ed., *Pre-
    Capitalist Economic Formations* (London: Lawrence & Wishart, 1965).
4. Samir Amin, *Unequal Development: An Essay on the Social Formations of
    Peripheral Capitalism* (New York: Monthly Review Press, 1976);
    Eurocentrism, second edition (New York: Monthly Review Press, 2009).

Index

absolute rent, 73–77, 79
accumulation: empiricist approach to,
   33; law of, 48; Marx on, 15–16;
   models of, 89–90; pace of, 17; simple model of, 18–22; unchanging
   real wages and, 23–28
agriculture, 72, 74; in history of
   England, 78–79; predates capitalism,
   97; in transition from feudalism into
   capitalism, 133
Algeria, 81
alienation: in capitalism, 113–14; Marx
   on, 64; in Sraffa's system, 43
Altvater, 101
America: development of agriculture in,
   79–80; Marx on colonization of, 132
American Revolution (1776), 115
Arrighi, Giovanni, 83

Bandung, 122–28
"Bandung era" (1955–1980), 89, 106
banks, 63; during financial crisis, 65
Banque de France, 63
Baran, Paul, 13, 26, 44, 117; on consumption of surplus value by state,
   27; on financialization, 65; on oligopolies, 28; on third department in
   capitalism, 49
bilateral monopoly, 99
Böhm-Bawerk, 43

bourgeoisie: in alliance with peasantry,
   80–81; in center and in periphery,
   92; in struggle against imperialism,
   123, 124
bubbles (economic), 65

Capital (*Das Kapital*; Marx): on law of
   value, 30; law of value in, 12; political economy of, 10; on prices of production, 31; publishing history of
   and gaps in, 131–36; on social
   classes, 61–62; on social reproduction, 44
capital equipment, 19–22, 25
capital goods, 25
capitalism, 130; cognitive capitalism,
   51–52; ecology versus, 103; economic laws of, 11; financial crises in,
   65; globalization of, 119–21; "green
   capitalism," 103; history of, 116–19,
   133; imperialism and, 84; instability
   of, 114–15; market alienation in,
   113–14; Marx on accumulation in,
   15–16; Marx's radical critique of, 9,
   132; monetary system of, 63;
   monopoly capitalism, 117–18; non-
   renewable resources under, 96–97;
   oligopolies in, 28–29; surplus value
   under, 32; third department in,
   49–50

CPSIA information can be obtained at www.ICGtesting.com
Printed in the USA
LVOW120830100613

337779LV00006B/472/P

9 781583 672334